130 NEW

WINEMAKING RECIPES

Make Delicious Wine at Home Using Fruits, Grains, and Herbs

C. J. J. Berry

FOX CHAPEL
PUBLISHING

Copyright © C. J. J. Berry, 1985, 2011.

First published in the United Kingdom by Argus Books, Ltd., 1985.
First published in North America in 2011, updated and revised, by Fox Chapel Publishing,
1970 Broad Street, East Petersburg, PA 17520.

ISBN 978-1-56523-600-4

Library of Congress Cataloging-in-Publication Data

Berry, Cyril J. J.
 130 new winemaking recipes / C. J. J. Berry.
   p. cm.
 Includes index.
 ISBN 978-1-56523-600-4
 1. Wine and wine making. I. Title. II. Title: One hundred thirty new winemaking recipes.
 TP548.B415 2011
 641.2'2--dc22
                                      2011009666

To learn more about the other great books from Fox Chapel Publishing, or to find a retailer near
you, call toll-free 800-457-9112 or visit us at *www.FoxChapelPublishing.com*.

Note to Authors: We are always looking for talented authors to write new books. Please send a
brief letter describing your idea to Acquisition Editor, 1970 Broad Street, East Petersburg, PA 17520.

Printed in China
First printing: October 2011

TABLE OF CONTENTS

Welcome to Winemaking

Nowadays, there is growing interest in winemaking, and thousands of people are discovering for themselves the truth of what I have been propounding for the last forty years, that winemaking is a really exciting and absorbing hobby, with an enjoyable "end product," to use the TV idiom.

Winemaking shops have made their appearance in most towns, and attractively packed winemaking kits can be bought in them, in chain stores, and online. There is certainly no difficulty nowadays in finding a supplier.

Many winemakers, however, want to take their winemaking beyond the making up of a simple kit according to the manufacturer's instructions— "winemaking by numbers." They want to be able to make their own wines from fruit or other ingredients garnered from their garden or from the hedgerows. It's more fun, and it's certainly a whole lot cheaper.

Legally, the United States federal government permits you to make as much 200 gallons (757 liters) of wine at home, but state laws vary as to whether you can transport that wine, sell it, or enter it in competitions.

Making wine at home is not difficult, despite what some of the experts say. Most of the utensils can be found in any kitchen—a large saucepan or kettle for boiling (stainless steel, aluminum, or sound enamel ware, but not iron, brass, or copper), a 7.5-quart (7 liter) or 10-quart (9 liter) white polythene bucket, a 25-quart (22.5 liter) white plastic fermenting bin (bucket), bottles and corks, and a stainless steel or polypropylene spoon.

Other items that will be found useful are glass 5-quart (4.5 liter) jars (the sort with ear handles), fermentation traps to keep the wine from contamination, a yard of acrylic tubing for siphoning, a corking tool, a large plastic funnel for filtering (the larger the better), and, if you wish to go further into the "mysteries," a hydrometer to help calculate the strength of your wines. This is dealt with in detail in *First Steps in Winemaking*.

Notice that your utensils, apart from the boiler and crock already mentioned, should be of glass, non-resinous wood (oak, ash, or beech), or high-density white plastic.

Cleanliness

Everything must be kept scrupulously clean by the use of boiling water or by the use of cleaning and sterilizing solutions on bottles and apparatus.

Cleaning solutions

Soda: 4 oz (125 g) washing soda in 5 quarts (4.5 liters) water.
Hypochlorite: 1 fl oz (30 ml) domestic bleach in 5 quarts (4.5 liters) water.
Rinse well afterwards in cold water in both cases.

Sterilizing solution

Six Campden tablets and ½ oz (15 g) citric acid in 20 fl oz (about ½ liter). Avoid inhaling. Rinse well afterwards.

Chempro is a marvelous proprietary cleaner/sterilizer used at 2 tablespoons per 5 quarts (4.5 liters).

What Wine Is

Any wine initially consists of: flavoring, water, sugar, acid, tannin, and yeast and nutrient. Another ingredient, which is perhaps the hardest to find, is time.

All that happens when yeast, a living organism, is put into a sugary solution, is that it feeds upon the sugar, converting it roughly half to alcohol and half to carbon dioxide, by weight, so that one finishes up with a pleasantly-flavored alcoholic drink.

We extract the flavor from fruits and vegetables by boiling them, by soaking them in cold water, or by a combination of the two (i.e., pouring boiling water on them and leaving them to soak). Or we can simply express the juice by means of a press or juice extractor and add the required amount of water.

An even simpler way to extract flavor is to buy a pectin-destroying enzyme such as Pectinol, Pektolase, or Rohament P, and add small quantities of this to the chopped-up fruit as directed. It will break down the fruit tissues and release the juice, which can then be strained off. It is a good idea to use this in most fruit wines.

In regards to sugar, one need only remember that 2 lb, 3 oz (about 1 kg) in 5 quarts (4.5 liters) will produce a dry wine of table strength; 2½ lb (1.1 kg) will produce a medium stronger wine, and sugar beyond that, and certainly beyond

3 lb (1.3 kg), will merely serve to make the wine sweeter, since it will not be converted to alcohol. Such sweetening sugar is better added in 4-oz (100 g) doses toward the end of the fermentation.

Note that there is a difference between in the gallon and to the gallon. "In the gallon" means that you have to have so much sugar and make the total volume up to 1 gallon. "To the gallon" means that you add your sugar to 1 gallon of water, and therefore finish up with more than 1 gallon. And, of course, you need more sugar (and ingredients) to achieve the same strength.

Yeast

There are many types of yeast. I would recommend either a good-quality wine yeast, liquid or granulated, obtainable from any winemaking shop. Sometimes, however, beginners like to use a baker's or brewer's yeast because it gives a more frothy, and therefore comforting, ferment, but the wine produced is not of such good quality. All will make wine, of varying quality, and usually the decision as to which type to use resolves itself into a matter of personal preference.

In all the following recipes, use a wine yeast or 1 level teaspoon of a good granulated yeast. With wine yeasts, full instructions are supplied.

Beware of "no yeast" recipes. No liquor will work without yeast; it means that you are relying upon the natural yeast in the fruit, or, if you have killed that by the use of boiling water or sulfite, on any "wild" yeast that happens to be in the air, and the gamble may not come off.

Nutrient

Yeast nutrient can be used to "boost" the action of the yeast and is particularly recommended in flower, mead, and other wines where the liquor is likely to be deficient in certain trace minerals. One can obtain nutrient ready made up, but why not make up your own from these chemicals (which you can buy, quite cheaply, from any winemaking shop or chemist)?

For 5 quarts (4.5 liters):

½ teaspoon ammonium phosphate

½ teaspoon ammonium sulfate

One 3-mg Vitamin B_1 tablet

Acid and Tannin

An important constituent of wine is acid, which can be included in the form of citric, tartaric, or malic acid. Citric acid is the most popular and, if you are formulating a recipe, include at least 1 level teaspoon with fruit wines and as much as 4 when using non-acid ingredients such as flowers or grain.

The inclusion of some tannin will make a marked improvement in many wines, giving them that desirable "bite" without which they can be "flabby" and uninteresting. Buy it at your wine shop and use only sparingly, as directed.

Fermentation

The fermentation should be in two stages. The first is a vigorous one when the yeast is multiplying itself to the required level and needs air for the process. For this, it is advisable to have your jar only three-quarters full, to allow room for frothing. For the second quieter stage, the jar is topped up with water and the air excluded, an unkind device that forces the yeast to produce more alcohol. This will act as a barrier to infection, and to the vinegar bacteria and other bugs that are the winemaker's biggest enemies. That is why one should employ the modern device of a fermentation lock at this stage.

Winemaking Summarized

1. Extract flavor from ingredients by pressing, boiling, or soaking in bowl or polythene bucket.

2. Add sugar and yeast and ferment for up to ten days in a polythene bucket or bin in a warm place 70°-75°F (20°-25°C).

3. Strain off, put into fermentation bottle, and fit fermentation trap, filling to within an inch (2.5 cm) of bottom of cork. Temperature: about 60°F (15°C). This fermentation will be much softer and will proceed for some weeks, but eventually all bubbling will cease.

4. Rack, i.e., siphon, the cleared wine off the lees (yeast deposit at the bottom of the jar). This should be repeated about a month later, and usually a third racking after a further three weeks is beneficial. By now the temperature should have been reduced to 60°F (15°C) and the wine should be quite stable, with no risk of explosions.

5. Bottle when wine is about six months old and cork securely. Bottles are then stored, preferably on their sides, in a room at about 55°F (13°C).

Do's and Don'ts

Do...

Keep things very clean.

Keep air away except during first few days, and even then, keep brew closely covered.

Use fermentation trap for secondary fermentation.

Keep fermenting bottles full to within 1 in (2.5 cm) of bottom of cork.

Strain wine well initially, or the wine will be hard to clarify.

Keep a book and jot down all you do so you can repeat it.

Use new corks.

Keep red wines in dark bottles to preserve their color.

Don't...

Allow infection to get at brew.

Forget to stir the "must" twice daily.

Ferment in a metal vessel.

Put wine in old damp bottles, or it may become infected.

Let sediment lie at bottom of jar, or it will impart a bad taste to the wine.

Rush a wine. Give it time!

Use finings or filter unnecessarily. Most wines will clear of their own accord, given time.

Use too much sugar, or your wines will be oversweet.

Favorite Wine Recipes

Almond (Calcavella) Wine

Mrs. Maie Davis of 4 Hampton Court, King's Lynn

Ingredients

* 1 lb (450 g) raisins
* 3 lemons
* 2¼ lb (1 kg) granulated sugar
* 2 oz (55 g) almonds (sweet, a few bitter may be added)
* Yeast and nutrient (she uses a Sauternes)
* Water to 5 quarts (4.5 liters)

Method

Chop the almonds and raisins and put them in muslin with the rind of the lemons. Boil gently in 110 fl oz (3 liters) water. Add the sugar, stirring to dissolve, and the juice of lemons. Cool to blood heat (98.6°F, 37°C) and add yeast. Ferment three to four days, then strain into 5-quart (4.5 liter) jar to ferment, top up to bottom of neck with cold water, and fit trap.

Apple Wine

Apples make a truly delicious table wine, in the making of which there are only two difficulties: the pulping and the pressing. Cutting up large quantities of apples with a knife is a tedious and blister-making business. Ideally, the problem is solved by means of one of the neat apple mills or juice extractors that can now be obtained. Failing this, however, the job can be almost equally comfortably tackled with a cutting board and a small kindling axe, holding it near the head and allowing the weight of the blade to do all the work. This is much easier than using a knife (the ancient Chinese knew a thing or two when they used heavy kitchen implements for chopping up food). A press for the pulp is a great help, but if you cannot buy, beg, or borrow one, wrap your apple pulp in stout cloths, place the "pudding" on a strong open framework or laths (an iron foot scraper or sieve) over a large vessel, and press upon it with your weight with your fists. This will extract most of the juice.

An even easier method is to break down the fruit with an anti-pectin enzyme, and then strain it through close-mesh nylon material.

The apples you use are important. The best eating apples do not make the best wine. Usually the "rougher" the apple, the better the result. Cider apples are ideal, cookers are a good second best, and 1 lb (½ kg) of crab apples in 10 will result in a great improvement. Russets are to be avoided, and a good plan is to use as big a mixture of types as possible.

If you have a real glut of apples, use as much as 24 lb (10 kg) to 5 quarts (4.5 liters) of water (the water will not cover them during mashing) and you will get a truly glorious wine. If you have fewer, use 12 lb (5 kg) for each 5 quarts (4.5 liters) and you will still get a delicious, but less full-bodied wine. The quantity can even be cut down to 6 lb (2.5 kg), but the general opinion is that then the flavor and body are not wholly satisfactory.

Ingredients

* 12-24 lb (5-10 kg) mixed apples
* 3 lb (1.3 kg) white sugar to 5 quarts (4.5 liters) of liquor
* 5 quarts (4.5 liters) water
* Yeast and nutrient
* Pectic enzyme

Method

Chop or crush the apples into small pieces, and put into a polythene bucket or trashcan. Add the water (cold), the pectic enzyme, and 2 level teaspoons of a granulated yeast. Leave for about a week, closely covered, stirring vigorously from the bottom at least twice a day to bring the lower apples to the top. This system breaks all the accepted rules in that the fruit is not sterilized, either with boiling water, or with sulfite, yet we have never known the recipe to fail. Keep the bucket in a fairly warm place, of course, then strain the juice from the pulp. Press the pulp as efficiently as you can and add the juice to the rest of the liquor. Measure, and for every 5 quarts (4.5 liters) add 4 lb (2 kg) of sugar. Put into cask or other fermenting vessel and fit fermentation lock, racking when it has cleared. The wine will probably be ready for drinking within six months, but is vastly improved by being matured in wood for a year. A further improvement can be effected by using a Sauternes yeast. If a really dry wine is required, reduce the sugar by ½ lb (225 g).

"Yes, you can make wine from almost anything..."

Apricot Sherry

Ingredients

- 1 lb (450 g) dried apricots
- 3 lb (1.3 kg) sugar
- 1 cup strong tea
- 96 fl oz (3 liters) water
- Sherry yeast (or wine yeast of choice) and yeast nutrient
- Pectic enzyme

Method

Wash the apricots well and slice. Add 96 fl oz (3 liters) of water and simmer for thirty minutes. Do not boil. Strain, add the sugar, and boil for a further five minutes. Add 10 fl oz (284 ml) of strong tea and pour all into a 5-quart (4.5 liter) jar. When cool, add the pectic enzyme. Twenty-four hours later, add the sherry culture or a level teaspoon of dried yeast, fit a fermentation lock in the neck of the jar, which should only be nine-tenths full, and set aside to ferment.

After a month, empty the liquid from the fermentation lock, but lightly plug its upper end with cotton wool and replace it, in order to give the sherry yeast the air it needs (if "ordinary" yeast is being used this is unnecessary).

Leave undisturbed for at least six months, then rack off into a clean jar together with a little of the cleanest yeast from the bottom of the vessel and bring into a warm room for a few days to speed the final fermentation. Top up with cold water, if necessary, to bottom of neck. When the fermentation has picked up, remove vessel to a cool spot and leave for a further six months before bottling. When a year old, it is a most satisfactory sherry-flavored wine.

BANANA WINE

INGREDIENTS

- 3 lb (1.3 kg) peeled bananas
- ½ lb (225 g) banana skins
- ¼ lb (100 g) raisins
- 2 lb (1 kg) sugar
- Yeast and nutrient
- Pectic enzyme
- 1 lemon, 1 orange
- Water to 5 quarts (4.5 liters)

METHOD

Use black or spotted bananas, whatever you can scrounge. Place bananas and fruit peel into a cloth bag and put the bag, tied up, into a large saucepan or boiler with 96 fl oz (3 liters) water. Bring to the boil, then gently simmer for half an hour. Pour the hot liquor over the sugar and fruit juice and, when the cloth bag has cooled, squeeze it with the hands to extract as much liquor as possible. When all the liquor is lukewarm, 70°F (20°C), add the yeast, pectic enzyme, and nutrient. Leave it in a warm place for a week, stirring daily, then pour into a glass jar and move it to a cooler place. It will be a thick-looking mess, like a lot of soapsuds. Keep it well covered and in a couple of months it will have a large sediment at the bottom. Siphon off, then add the chopped raisins. Top up to bottom of neck with cold water if necessary. Fit an air lock and siphon off again after four months. By then it will have started to clear. Leave a further six months before sampling. It improves the longer you keep it.

Spiced Banana Wine

Ingredients

- 3 lb (1.5 kg) bananas (including skins) or 6 oz (170 g) dried variety
- 1 oz (30 g) cloves
- 1 oz (30 g) ginger
- 2½ lb (1.25 kg) sugar
- ½ oz (15 g) citric acid (or 3 lemons, no pith, in lieu)
- 1½ pints (500 ml) strong tea (a teaspoon of grape tannin)
- 6 pints (3.5 liters) water
- Yeast nutrient and activated wine yeast

Method

Thinly slice the bananas and skins. Place these into the initial fermentation bin or bucket together with sugar, cloves, and ginger, and pour in boiling water. Stir to dissolve the sugar, and when cool, add the citric acid and strong tea. Introduce the activated wine yeast and nutrient. Ferment on the fruit for ten days, then strain into fermentation jar. Fit airlock and ferment to a finish in the normal way, racking as necessary in due course.

DRIED BANANAS

INGREDIENTS

- 12 oz (335 g) dried bananas
- 8 oz (225 g) raisins
- 2 level teaspoons citric acid
- 2 lb, 3 oz (about 1 kg) sugar
- Pectic enzyme
- 1 sherry yeast (liquid or dry, or wine yeast of choice)
- Water to 5 quarts (4.5 liters)

METHOD

Simmer the dried bananas in the pressure cooker for ten minutes, then put into fermenting bucket and make up to 96 fl oz (3 liters) with cold water. Add the raisins, citric acid, and sugar. When quite cool, add the pectin destroying enzyme and, twenty-four hours later, the yeast. Ferment on the pulp for seven days, stirring every day and keeping closely covered.

Strain into a 5-quart (4.5 liter) jar, make up to 5 quarts (4.5 liters) with a little cold water, and ferment under the protection of a fermentation lock in the usual manner.

Banana and Dried Elderberry

Ingredients

- 2 lb (1 kg) bananas (including skins) or 4 oz (100 g) dried variety
- 1 lb (450 g) dried elderberries
- 3 lb (1.3 kg) sugar
- ½ oz (15 g) citric acid (or 3 lemons, no pith, in lieu)
- A pinch of grape tannin
- 112 fl oz (3.5 liters) water
- Yeast nutrient and wine yeast

Method

Slice up the bananas thinly, including skins, and place in the initial fermentation bucket, together with the dried elderberries and sugar. Pour in boiling water and stir until sugar is dissolved. When cool, add the citric acid and tannin. Introduce the yeast nutrient and activated wine yeast and leave to ferment on the fruit for ten days, then siphon into fermentation jar and top up to bottom of neck if necessary. Fit airlock and leave to ferment in normal way, racking as necessary in due course.

BANANA AND FIG WINE

INGREDIENTS

- 2 lb (1 kg) bananas (including skins) or 3 oz (100 g) dried variety
- 2 lb (1 kg) dried figs
- 3 lb (1.3 kg) sugar
- ½ oz (15 g) citric acid (or 3 lemons, no pith, in lieu)
- A pinch of grape tannin
- 96 fl oz (3 liters) water
- Yeast nutrient and activated wine yeast
- Pectic enzyme

METHOD

Chop the bananas and skins into small thin pieces. Similarly chop the dried figs and place these together with the sugar into a polythene bucket or bin. Pour the boiling water over the chopped fruit and then stir well. When cool, add citric acid, tannin, and pectic enzyme. Twenty-four hours later, introduce the yeast nutrient and activated wine yeast. Ferment on the pulp for ten days, closely covered, then strain into fermentation jar. Top up with a little cold water if necessary. Fit airlock and allow to ferment in normal way. Rack as necessary in due course.

BANANA AND PARSNIP WINE

INGREDIENTS

- 2 lb (1 kg) bananas (including skins) or 3 oz (100 g) dried variety
- 4 lb (2 kg) parsnips
- 3 lb (1.3 kg) sugar
- ½ oz (15 g) citric acid or (3 lemons, no pith, in lieu)
- A pinch of grape tannin
- 96 fl oz (3 liters) water
- Yeast nutrient and activated wine yeast
- Pectic enzyme

METHOD

Scrub and thinly slice parsnips and boil slowly until tender, then pour the extract over the chopped bananas and skins. Add the sugar and stir until dissolved. When cool, add the citric acid, tannin, and pectic enzyme. Twenty-four hours later, introduce the activated wine yeast and nutrient, and ferment on the banana pulp for ten days. Strain into fermentation jar and top up to bottom of neck, if necessary, with cold water. Fit airlock and allow to ferment in the normal way, racking into clean jar when it clears.

"...and now may I introduce your Chairman..."

BANANA AND PRUNE WINE

INGREDIENTS

- 2 lb (1 kg) bananas (including skins) or 4 oz (100 g) dried variety
- 2 lb (1 kg) sugar
- 2 lb (1 kg) prunes
- ½ lb (225 g) raisins
- ½ oz (15 g) citric acid or (3 lemons, no pith, in lieu)
- A pinch of grape tannin
- 112 fl oz (3.5 liters) water
- Pectic enzyme
- Yeast nutrient and activated wine yeast

METHOD

Thinly slice the bananas and skins. Also slice the prunes in half. Place into the initial fermentation bucket and add the chopped raisins and sugar. Pour in the boiling water and stir until sugar is dissolved. When cool, add the citric acid, tannin, and pectic enzyme. Next day, introduce the yeast nutrient and activated wine yeast. Ferment on the pulp for ten days, then strain into fermentation jar and top up with cold water. Fit air lock and leave to ferment in normal way, racking as necessary in due course.

Banana and Rice

Ingredients

- 2 lb (1 kg) bananas (including skins) or 3 oz (100 g) dried variety
- 3 lb (1.3 kg) paddy rice (with husk)
- ½ lb (225 g) stoned raisins
- 3 lb (1.3 kg) sugar
- ½ oz (15 g) citric acid (or 3 lemons, no pith, in lieu)
- A pinch of grape tannin
- 136 fl oz (4 liters) water
- Yeast and nutrient
- Pectic enzyme

Method

Place the finely chopped bananas and skins, paddy rice, and stoned raisins, together with the sugar, into a polythene bin or bucket. Pour in the boiling water and stir until sugar is dissolved. When cool, add the citric acid, tannin, and enzyme. Next day, introduce the yeast nutrient and activated wine yeast and ferment for ten days on the pulp. Strain into fermentation jar. Top up the jar with cold water, if necessary, fit airlock, and ferment to completion in the normal way, racking as necessary in due course.

Banana and Rose Hip Shell Wine

Ingredients

- 2 lb (1 kg) bananas (including skins) or 3 oz (100 g) dried variety
- ½ lb (225 g) dried rose hips, 3 oz (100 g) rose hip shells (A handful of hawthorn berries or (some) dried elderberries will give this wine an excellent color)
- 3 lb (1.3 kg) sugar
- ½ oz (15 g) citric acid
- A pinch of grape tannin
- 136 fl oz (4 liters) water
- Yeast nutrient and activated wine yeast
- Pectic enzyme

Method

Chop the bananas and skins into thin slices and pour boiling water over them. Add sugar and stir until dissolved. The rose hips, hawthorn berries, and elderberries, indeed all three if desired, should then be added. When cool, add citric acid, tannin, and pectic enzyme. Twenty-four hours later, introduce the yeast nutrient and activated wine yeast and ferment for ten days on the pulp. Strain into fermentation jar and top up with cold water. Fit air lock and ferment in the normal way, racking as necessary in due course.

"...he does an awful lot of wine judging..."

Dried Banana and Rose Hip

Ingredients

- 3 oz (100 g) rose hip shells
- 12 oz (350 g) dried bananas
- Pectic enzyme
- 2 teaspoons citric acid
- 2 lb, 3 oz (about 1 kg) sugar
- A wine yeast and nutrient
- Water to 5 quarts (4.5 liters)

Method

Bring 2.5 quarts (2 liters) of water to the boil and pour over the rose hip shells. Simmer the dried bananas in another 2.5 quarts (2 liters) water in the pressure cooker for ten minutes. Mix the two lots and add the citric acid and sugar. Stir well. When cool, about 70°F (20°C), add the pectic enzyme and a few hours later the yeast and nutrient. Ferment on the pulp for seven days, stirring every day. Strain off into a 5-quart (4.5 liter) jar, top up with water, fit air lock, and ferment under a fermentation lock until clear, in the usual manner. Siphon into a clean jar. Leave for a further three months before bottling.

BANANA AND SARSAPARILLA

INGREDIENTS

- 3 lb (1.3 kg) bananas (including skins) or 6 oz (170 g) dried variety
- 2 oz (55 g) sarsaparilla
- 2 lb, 11 oz (1.2 kg) sugar
- ½ oz (15 g) citric acid (or 3 lemons, no pith, in lieu)
- A teaspoon grape tannin
- 136 fl oz (4 liters) water
- Yeast nutrient and activated wine yeast

METHOD

Thinly slice the bananas and skins and place in the initial fermentation vessel. Add the sugar and pour in boiling water. Stir to dissolve, then add the sarsaparilla. When cool, add the citric acid and tannin. Introduce the yeast nutrient and activated wine yeast. Ferment on the pulp for ten days, then strain into fermentation jar and top up with cold water. Fit air lock and ferment to a finish in the normal way, racking as necessary in due course.

"That last lot of wine seems extra gassy!"

Barley and Other Grain Wines

Once the main rush of the winemaking season is over, why not make a good stock of cereal wine? The usual favorites are barley, wheat, or corn, although some like rice, and they can all be made from the same basic recipe, using 1 lb (450 g) of grain. Barley gives the smoothest wine with most body, corn is intermediate in this respect, and wheat wine tends to be thinner and have more bite, and is often said to have a slight whisky flavor (although not, of course, whisky strength).

Ingredients

* 1 lb (450 g) barley, corn, or wheat
* 2 lb, 8 oz (1.1 kg) white sugar
* 1 lb (450 g) raisins
* 2 lemons, 1 orange
* Yeast nutrient
* Water to 5 quarts (4.5 liters)

Method

Wash the grain, then soak it overnight in 16 fl oz (500 ml) of the water. The next day, mince both grain and raisins in a domestic mincer (using the coarsest holes) and put into a crock or bowl with the sugar and the thinly pared rinds of the fruit. Pour over them 136 fl oz (4 liters) of boiling water. Cover. Cool to tepid, 70°F (20°C), then add the juice of the lemons and orange, the yeast, and yeast nutrient. Cover closely and leave in a warm place, 65°-70°F (17°-20°C), for a week, stirring daily. Strain into a fermenting jar, topping up with cold water if necessary, and fit air lock. Siphon off the lees when it clears and refit lock. Leave for a further three months or so before racking into clean bottles,

When making rice wine, use the above recipe, but use 3 lb (1.3 kg) of rice instead of 1 lb (450 g).

BEETROOT WINE

This recipe uses young beetroot, and the secret is to make sure that they are not over boiled.

INGREDIENTS

- 4 lb (2 kg) young beetroot
- 2½ lb (1.2 kg) sugar
- Yeast and nutrient
- 1 lemon
- 4 to 6 cloves
- ½ oz (15 g) root ginger
- Water to 5 quarts (4.5 liters)

METHOD

Wash the beetroot thoroughly, then slice thinly. Bring to the boil in 112 fl oz (3.5 liters) of water with the thinly peeled rind of the lemon, the cloves, and the ginger. Simmer until the beetroot is tender and loses its color. Strain onto the sugar, preferably in a polythene bucket. Stir well to dissolve, and when lukewarm, 70°F (20°C), add the juice of the lemon and the yeast (a pre-prepared wine yeast or a level teaspoon of granulated yeast). Cover and leave in a warm place, 65°-70°F (17°-20°C), for two days to begin fermentation. Then pour into fermenting vessel, topping up with cold water, and fit fermentation trap. Siphon off when it clears, and bottle when stable in dark bottles to preserve its color.

"Say if it's too strong for you..."

Beetroot and Parsnip Wine
C. Shave

Ingredients

- 2 lb (1 kg) frosted parsnips
- 2 lb (1 kg) old beetroot
- 2½ lb (1.2 kg) sugar
- Grape tannin
- Pectic enzyme
- 2 lemons
- 2 oranges or ½ oz (15 g) citric acid
- Yeast nutrient
- Yeast (selected wine or general purpose)
- Water to 5 quarts (4.5 liters)

Method

Wash the roots well (do not peel), slice thinly, and place in 112 fl oz (3.5 liters) of water with the grated peel (no white pith) of the fruit and the tea. Simmer until the roots are tender. (Any over-boiling may result in a cloudy wine). Strain and dissolve the sugar in the liquor. When cool, add the pectic enzyme and, twenty-four hours later, the yeast. Thereafter, continue as for beetroot wine.

"Can't think where that judge has got to."

BEET AND PINEAPPLE WINE

This is an unusual combination, but it makes an excellent wine. The recipe is that of Mrs. M. Paton, of Muirend, Stewarton, Kilmarnock, Ayrshire.

INGREDIENTS

- 4 lb (2 kg) beets
- 1 lb (450 g) raisins
- 2 lb, 3 oz (about 1 kg) sugar
- 1 large or 2 small pineapples
- 2 lemons
- Yeast
- Water to 5 quarts (4.5 liters)

METHOD

Wash the beets, but do not peel them, and cut into small pieces. Peel pineapples thickly. Put peel of pineapples and cut-up beets into pan, cover with 112 fl oz (3.5 liters) of water, and boil till beet is tender, but not mushy. (The remainder of the pineapples can be eaten.) Put sugar, raisins (washed and chopped), and sliced lemons into bucket, and strain the hot liquor over them, stirring to dissolve the sugar. Allow to cool to 70°F (20°C), then add the yeast (and, preferably, some nutrient for it), cover with a thick cloth, and stand in a warm place to ferment. After five days or so, strain into fermenting jar, top up to bottom of neck with cold water, and fit trap. Rack off and bottle when wine has completely cleared. If after a while it throws a sediment, rack again. As an alternative, use 3 lb (1.3 kg) beets and 1 lb (450 g) black grapes. Crush the grapes and add them to the sugar, raisins, etc., in the bucket. Use dark bottles.

Blackberry Wine

Ingredients

- 3 lb (1.3 kg) blackberries
- 2 lb, 11 oz (1.2 kg) sugar
- 136 fl oz (4 liters) water
- Yeast and nutrient

Method

Pick the blackberries when they are fully ripe, and use only those of the best quality. Crush them in a plastic bucket with a stainless steel or wooden spoon and add water, mixing thoroughly. Allow them to stand overnight, then strain them through a nylon sieve onto the sugar, and stir well to dissolve. Add yeast and nutrient, cover closely with a sheet of polythene or thick cloth, and leave in a warm place 70°-75°F (20°-25°C) for a week. Then, when the first vigorous ferment has subsided, stir and transfer to fermenting jar. Fit fermentation lock and place in an area with a temperature of 60°-65°F (15°-17°C) for the main fermentation. If possible, use an opaque colored jar, but if you have only a white or clear glass one, wrap it in brown paper or keep it away from the light to preserve the wine's glorious ruby color. You may have to top up a little with cold water. Rack for the first time after three months, refitting air lock, and again into clean colored bottles when the wine is finished (about two months later).

BLACKBERRY WINE

INGREDIENTS

- 5 lb (2.5 kg) blackberries
- 2½ lb (1.2 kg) sugar
- 136 fl oz (4 liters) water
- Yeast
- Pectic enzyme

METHOD

Wash the berries thoroughly in a colander, then crush them in a bowl and pour over them 136 fl oz (4 liters) of water, boiling. Allow them to steep for two days, then strain the liquor through a nylon sieve onto the sugar, stir well to dissolve, and add the pectic enzyme. Twenty-four hours later, add yeast. Leave for five or six days, well covered, then pour into fermenting jar, filling to shoulder, and fit trap. Thereafter continue as usual. This makes a full-bodied sweet wine.

"And there are two I keep for my personal use."

Black Currant Wine

Ingredients

- 3 lb (1.3 kg) black currants
- 2¼ lb (1 kg) sugar
- 136 fl oz (4 liters) water
- Yeast and nutrient

Method

Strip any stems from the fruit and wash it well. Crush in a polythene bucket with a wooden spoon, and then proceed as for cherry and blackberry wines.

This makes a pleasant, dry, and fairly light table wine. A wine with greater body and correspondingly greater sweetness can be made by increasing the weight of fruit up to 4.5 lb (about 2 kg) with 112 fl oz (3.5 liters) of water and by using 3 lb (1.3 kg) of sugar.

In this case, pour all the water, boiling, over the crushed fruit. Allow to stand for twenty-four hours, then strain off the liquor and add the sugar. Ferment, rack, and bottle as usual.

BROOM OR COLTSFOOT WINE

This same recipe can also be used for coltsfoot and many similar flower wines. It is not now recommended, though, that primroses or cowslips be used for winemaking, owing to their increasing scarcity.

The same basic recipe can be used for each of these wines, and the most important single point to note is that it is essential, if a wine of good strength is required, to use yeast nutrient. Since these are "ladies' wines," they may be preferred sweet, and I would suggest using 3 lb (1.3 kg) of sugar, but anyone preferring a medium or dry wine should reduce this quantity to 2½ lb (1.2 kg) and 2 lb (1 kg) respectively. Broom wine is certainly the better for having only 2½ lb (1.2 kg) of sugar.

INGREDIENTS

- 5 quarts (4.5 liters) broom or coltsfoot (heads only)
- 3 lb (1.3 kg) white sugar
- 2 oranges, 1 lemon
- Yeast and nutrient
- Water to 5 quarts (4.5 liters)

METHOD

Bring 136 fl oz (4 liters) of water to the boil and stir the sugar into it, making sure that it is all dissolved. Put the peel of the fruit (but no white pith) into a bowl or polythene bucket and pour the hot syrup over it. Allow the liquor to cool to 70°F (20°C) before adding the flowers, fruit juice, yeast, and yeast nutrient. (If delicate flowers are put into boiling water the wine is usually spoiled.) Cover closely and leave in a warm place for seven days, stirring each day. Then strain through a nylon sieve (or muslin) into a fermenting jar, topping up with cold water to the bottom of the neck, and fit a fermentation lock. Leave it in a warm place for three months, by which time there will be an appreciable and firm yeast deposit. Siphon the wine off the lees into a clean jar for another three months, when it can be racked again, this time into bottles if desired.

Bullace Wine

Bullaces, or bullace plums, are seen in some gardens and grow wild in many areas, but many winemakers, seeing them for the first time, wonder what they are, although rightly sensing that they will make excellent wine. The best description one can give of them is that they are a cross between a plum and a sloe, both in size and appearance.

Ingredients

* 4 lb (2 kg) bullaces
* 2½ lb (1.2 kg) sugar
* ½ lb (225 g) raisins
* Pectic enzyme
* Yeast and nutrient
* Water to 5 quarts (4.5 liters)

Method

Crush the fruit to a pulp with a piece of hardwood and pour over it 112 fl oz (3.5 liters) of water, boiling. Cover with a cloth until cool, then add the pectic enzyme and leave for five days, stirring once or twice a day. Strain through a nylon sieve, pressing with a wooden spoon to express as much juice as possible, and dissolve the sugar in it. Chop the raisins, put them in a colander, and pour some boiling water over them to sterilize them. Then place them in a wide-necked fermentation vessel. Add the liquor, the yeast nutrient, and your chosen yeast. Cover the mouth of the jar with a sheet of polythene secured with a rubber band and leave in a temperature of 65°-70°F (17°-20°C). When the wine has cleared appreciably and a deposit of yeast has appeared (about two months), strain into fresh jar, top up to bottom of neck with cold water, and fit fermentation trap. Rack once more after a further three months, and bottle. Use opaque or dark glass vessels throughout so that the wine will retain its color.

CABBAGE WINE

INGREDIENTS

- 2 lb (1 kg) cabbage, including stalks
- 2¼ lb (1.1 kg) sugar
- 1 lb (450 g) crushed wheat, rice, or barley
- ½ lb (225 g) minced raisins (scalded)
- 8 fl oz (250 ml) cold tea
- 3 oranges or lemons (½ oz, 15 g, citric acid may be used in lieu)
- Activated yeast and nutrient
- Water to 5 quarts (4.5 liters)

METHOD

Mince the cabbage (including stalks) together with the grains (which should have been soaked overnight), the scalded raisins, and rinds (no pith) from the fruit. Place in fermentation vessel and add sugar. Add 136 fl oz (4 liters) of boiling water and stir to dissolve the sugar. When cool, add the cold tea, fruit juices (or citric acid), activated yeast, and nutrient. Ferment for seven days, then strain into glass jar. Fit fermentation lock, ferment, and rack in the normal way.

Carum Carvi Wine (Caraway Seed and Tea)

Ingredients

- 1 oz (30 g) packet caraway seed
- 1 lb (450 g) raisins or 16 fl oz (500 ml) grape concentrate
- ½ oz (15 g) citric acid (or 3 lemons, no pith, in lieu)
- 2½ lb (1.2 kg) sugar
- 1 quart (1 liter) weak tea
- Yeast nutrient and activated wine yeast

Method

Add the caraway seed to 96 fl oz (3 liters) of boiling water and bring this to a boil with the object of extracting the flavor from the seed. Strain over sugar and stir until dissolved. Chop the raisins and, after scalding, add to the sugared caraway solution. When cool, add the citric acid, cold tea, and introduce the yeast nutrient and activated wine yeast. Ferment on the pulp for seven days, then strain into fermenting vessel and ferment under airlock until it clears, then rack for the first time. Bottle when completely clear (about three-quarters of a month later).

CARVI FRUCTUS

INGREDIENTS

- 1 oz (30 g) caraway seeds
- 1 lb (450 g) crushed barley, wheat, or corn
- 2 lb (1 kg) green gooseberries or stoned raisins
- ½ oz (15 g) citric acid or 3 lemons (no pith)
- ¹⁄₁₀ oz (5 g) grape tannin
- 2½ lb (1.2 kg) sugar
- Yeast nutrient and activated yeast
- Water to 5 quarts (4.5 liters)

METHOD

Pour 136 fl oz (4 liters) of boiling water over the caraway seeds, crushed grains, and sugar. Stir well to dissolve the sugar, then add the crushed fruit. When cool, add grape tannin, citric acid, nutrient, and activated yeast. Ferment on solids for seven to ten days, stirring well each day, then strain into fermentation glass jar and top up with a little cold water if necessary. Fit airlock, ferment to a finish, and rack in the usual way.

Got quite a kick, hasn't it?

CARNATION WINE

INGREDIENTS

- 2 quarts (2 liters) white "pinks"
- 2½ lb (1.2 kg) sugar
- 1 orange
- 1 lemon
- ½ lb (225 g) raisins
- Yeast and nutrient
- Water to 5 quarts (4.5 liters)

METHOD

The delightful scent of these flowers does carry over into the wine and give it an attractive bouquet, which will particularly appeal to ladies (most men seem to prefer less scented wines). It is easy to make.

Put the flower heads into a bucket and pour over them 136 fl oz (4 liters) of water, boiling. Leave for not more than three days, giving an occasional stir. Strain and squeeze out the flowers lightly. Chop the raisins and slice the fruit thinly. Add them, with the sugar and yeast nutrient, to the liquor. Stir well to dissolve the sugar. Finally, add your yeast (a wine yeast or a level teaspoon of granulated yeast). Ferment in a temperature of 65°-70°F (17°-20°C) for ten days, keeping your bucket closely covered, then strain into a fermenting bottle and fit airlock. When the wine clears and there is a firm yeast sediment, rack into a clean jar and keep for another three months, this time corked, before the final bottling. It will be usable after about four months in bottle.

CARROT WINE

INGREDIENTS

- 3½ lb (1.6 kg) carrots
- 2½ lb (1.2 kg) granulated sugar
- Yeast and nutrient
- ½ oz (15 g) hops
- Water to 5 quarts (4.5 liters)

METHOD

Scrub the carrots well and chop them up. Put them in 96 fl oz (3 liters) of water, bring to the boil, and simmer until tender. Strain the liquid into another saucepan or boiler (throw away or eat the carrots), and add the sugar and hops. Stir well to dissolve the sugar and just bring the liquor to the boil. Allow to cool and strain into a bucket through a nylon sieve. When the temperature has dropped to about 70°F (20°C), add yeast, preferably a pre-activated wine yeast, and some yeast nutrient to give it a boost. If you are using a 5-quart (4.5 liter) jar, do not fill right up to the bottom of the neck in case the fermentation proves too vigorous. Keep a little of the liquor aside in a milk bottle plugged with cotton wool. Keep the jar in a warm place, with an airlock fitted. After five or six days, the ferment will have quieted and it can be topped right up from the bottle. Leave until the wine is clearing and a sediment has formed, then siphon it off the lees. Repeat this two to three months later when the wine is completely clear and bottle.

"Perhaps just a LEETLE too acidic!"

CHAMOMILE WINE
(Anthemis nobilis)

INGREDIENTS

- Chamomile flowers (18 or so)
- 4 lb (2 kg) carrots (swede or turnip if desired)
- ½ oz (15 g) citric acid (or 3 lemons, no pith, in lieu)
- 2½ lb (1.2 kg) sugar
- A pinch of grape tannin
- Yeast nutrient and activated wine yeast
- Water to 5 quart (4.5 liters)

METHOD

Scrub the carrot roots, but do not peel. Slice thinly into 112 fl oz (3.5 liters) of cold water and boil until tender and strain onto sugar. Stir until dissolved. Pour 1 quart (1 liter) of boiling water onto chamomile flowers and steep, as making tea. Add the strained infusion to the sugared root juice. When cool, add the citric acid, cold tea, yeast nutrient, and activated wine yeast. Ferment under an airlock until it clears, then rack for the first time. Bottle when completely clear (about three-quarters of a month later).

"But I only showed him around."

CHERRY WINE

INGREDIENTS

- 6 lb (3 kg) black cherries (weighed whole)
- 136 fl oz (4 liters) water
- 3½ lb (1.6 kg) granulated sugar
- 1 Campden tablet
- Yeast and nutrient

METHOD

Weigh the cherries whole, then remove stems, wash, and stone fruit. Crush the cherries in a bowl. Bring 80 fl oz (2.5 liters) of the water to the boil and pour over them. Cover closely with a sheet of polythene secured by elastic, or with a thick cloth, and leave for twenty-four hours. Then strain the liquor through a nylon sieve, or two thicknesses of muslin, and throw away the pulp after pressing out as much juice as possible. Bring the other 48 fl oz (1.5 liters) of water to the boil and dissolve the sugar in it, then add this syrup to the liquid already obtained. When the whole has cooled to just tepid, 70°F (20°C), add the yeast and nutrient and leave in a bowl or polythene bucket for ten days, closely covered as before, in a warm place 65°-70°F (17°-20°C). Then transfer it to a glass fermenting jar, topping up to the bottom of the neck if necessary with cold boiled water, and fit fermentation lock. Leave until all fermentation has ceased, then rack into clean jar. Rack again into bottles about two months later. This makes a delicious medium-sweet dessert wine.

Cherry Wine

Ingredients

- 4 lb (2 kg) sweet cherries (either black or red)
- 2½ lb (1.2 kg) white sugar
- Pectic enzyme
- 1 Campden tablet
- Yeast and nutrient
- Water to 5 quarts (4.5 liters)

Method

Use only ripe fruit. Avoid any that is moldy or damaged, or it may spoil the wine. Wash the fruit, chop it, place it in a bowl, and pour 112 fl oz (3 liters) of cold water over it. Add the Campden tablet and, twenty-four hours later, the pectic enzyme. Allow the fruit to steep (well covered) for four days. Then place the sugar in a bowl or crock and strain the juice onto it, either through a nylon sieve, or through a jelly bag or heavy cloth, squeezing well to express all possible juice. Stir well to dissolve the sugar, then add the yeast and yeast nutrient and pour into fermenting vessel. Ferment and rack in the usual way, topping up with cold water to the bottom of the neck when the first vigor of the fermentation dies down. Cherry wine made in this way will not have the deepness of color that is obtained by extracting the juice by using heat, but it will have an infinitely better flavor, that of the fresh fruit, and additional color can easily be added, if desired, to the finished wine by using a little fresh red fruit juice or purchased cherry coloring.

CLARY WINE

This is a favorite wine in many parts of the country, and is made from the blue flowers of clary sage. Clary is a member of the sage family, and the blue blossoms are gathered, if possible, just before they show signs of deteriorating, which is generally in late summer. This recipe will make a medium-sweet delicate wine.

INGREDIENTS

- 50 fl oz (1.5 liters) clary sage blossoms (or 1 package dried blossoms)
- 2¾ lb (1.2 kg) sugar
- 1 lb (450 g) raisins
- 2 lemons
- Yeast and nutrient
- Water to 5 quarts (4.5 liters)

METHOD

If you are using the dried blossoms obtained from an herbalist, it will be necessary to infuse for twenty-four hours before use. Boil the sugar in 112 fl oz (3.5 liters) of water for a few minutes and ensure that it is all well dissolved, then pour the hot liquor over the clary blossoms, the chopped raisins, and the juice and thin rinds (no pith) of the lemons. When the temperature has dropped to 70°F (20°C), add the yeast (a wine yeast or a level teaspoon of granulated yeast) and some yeast nutrient. Cover closely and stand in a warm place for a week to ferment. Stir well each day. After that period, remove the flowers, but leave the raisins in the liquor for a further ten days before straining into a fermenting jar, topping up with cold water, and fitting trap. Rack the wine for the first time when the top half is clear, and again about two months later when it has cleared completely.

Coffee Wine
W. Beavis, Southend

Ingredients

- 2 tablespoons coffee
- 2½ lb (1.2 kg) sugar
- 2 lemons
- Yeast and nutrient
- Water to 5 quarts (4.5 liters)

Method

Peel the lemons thinly, avoiding the white pith (a grater is the ideal way), and boil the peel in 112 fl oz (3.5 liters) of water with the coffee for half an hour. Strain onto the sugar and stir well to dissolve. Allow to cool and add the yeast, nutrient, and strained juice of the lemons. Cover closely and leave in a temperature of 65°-70°F (17°-20°C) for about a week before transferring to a 5-quart (4.5 liter) fermenting jar and fitting air lock. Top up with cold boiled water or syrup. Leave to ferment right out, then transfer to a cool place 55°-60°F (13°C) and siphon off the lees into clean bottles when it is completely clear.

CRAB APPLE WINE

INGREDIENTS

- 8 lb (4 kg) crab apples
- 5 fl oz (150 ml) grape concentrate (or 1 lb (450 g) raisins)
- 1 lb (450 g) wheat
- 2¼ lb (about 1 kg) sugar
- Yeast and nutrient
- Pectic enzyme
- Water to 5 quarts (4.5 liters)

METHOD

Wash the crab apples, then chop or crush them, and cover them with 136 fl oz (3.7 liters) of water. Add the pectic enzyme, a level teaspoon of granulated yeast, and some yeast nutrient and stir in well. Cover closely and leave in a warm place about 70°F (20°C), stirring well each day and mashing the apples with the hand for seven days.

By this time, the yeast will be fully active and much increased, so stir well, then strain through a nylon sieve. Enough yeast will be carried over to continue the ferment. Stir in the sugar, the grape concentrate or the chopped raisins, and the wheat. Cover closely and leave in a warm place to ferment for fourteen days. Strain into a fermenting jar, top with cold water, and fit airlock. Leave until the wine clears and there is a firm sediment, then siphon it off the lees into a fresh jar and refit trap. Leave for a further three months before racking again, this time into clean bottles.

CRAB APPLE WINE

INGREDIENTS

- 8 lb (3.6 kg) crab apples
- 3 lb (1.3 kg) sugar
- 5 quarts (4.5 liters) water
- Yeast and nutrient
- Pectic enzyme

METHOD

Put the crab apples in 136 fl oz (3.7 liters) of water and leave for three or four days (until they are well soaked), then mash them with the hand or a hardwood pulper and add the pectic enzyme, yeast, and nutrient. Leave another two weeks (closely covered, of course) stirring daily, then strain the liquor onto the sugar and stir well to dissolve. If you have any kind of press, it pays dividends to extract all possible juice from the pulp. Stir well to dissolve all the sugar, put into fermenting jar, and fit trap. Top up if necessary. Siphon off the lees into clean bottles when clear.

CURRANT WINE

INGREDIENTS

- 3 lb (1.3 kg) currants
- ½ lb (225 g) mixed minced peel
- ½ lb (225 g) barley
- 2½ lb (1.2 kg) sugar
- Yeast and nutrient
- Water to 5 quarts (4.5 liters)

METHOD

Bring 112 fl oz (3.5 liters) of water to the boil, add the currants, peel, and barley, and simmer for fifteen minutes. Strain onto the sugar and stir well to dissolve. When the liquor has cooled to tepid, 70°F (20°C), add a vigorous yeast and yeast nutrient. Pour the whole into a fermenting jar and fit trap. When the first frothy vigor of the ferment dies down, top up with cold water to the bottom of the neck. Leave to ferment out and siphon off the lees when it clears. Refit trap and leave till wine is stable, then bottle.

"I think I use rather too much of the main ingredient."

CURRANT AND RAISIN WINE

INGREDIENTS

- 2 lb (1 kg) currants
- 2 lb (1 kg) raisins
- 1 orange
- 1 lemon
- 1 lb (450 g) rice
- 2¾ lb (1.2 kg) sugar
- Yeast and nutrient
- 5 quarts (4.5 liters) water

METHOD

Bring 112 fl oz (3.5 liters) of water to the boil, add the currants, raisins, and orange peel, and simmer for twenty minutes. Strain, add the rice, and simmer for four minutes. Strain onto the sugar and stir thoroughly to dissolve it. When the liquor has cooled to 70°F (20°C), add the juice of the orange and lemon, the yeast, and some yeast nutrient. Pour into fermenting jar and fit air lock. Ferment out, rack, and bottle in the usual way. A variation is to use 4 lb (2 kg) currants, 1 lb (450 g) raisins, and 2¼ lb (about 1 kg) sugar. This will give a drier wine.

"Just a little YOUNG, perhaps?"

DAMSON WINE

Beware of recipes found in some books that tell you to boil damsons, for if you overdo it, you will release pectin into the wine, which will either cause it to jell or make it almost impossible to clear. These are the most common faults with plum wines. It is far better just to pour the boiling water over the fruit.

INGREDIENTS

- 4 lb (2 kg) damsons (or 6 lb (2.7 kg) for really good body)
- 3 lb (1.3 kg) sugar
- Yeast and nutrient
- Pectic enzyme
- Water to 5 quarts (4.5 liters)

METHOD

Put 112 fl oz (3.5 liters) of water on to boil, then crush the damsons in a bowl or bucket with half the sugar. Pour the boiling water over them, stir well to dissolve the sugar, and allow to cool to about 75°F (25°C) before adding the pectic enzyme, yeast, and yeast nutrient. Cover closely and leave for forty-eight hours in a warm place to allow the ferment to get well under way. Put the remaining sugar in a polythene bucket or other vessel and strain the liquor onto it. In this case, a nylon sieve or muslin is often not fine enough, and it pays to use a jelly bag or roll the pulp to and fro in nylon netting to be sure of the wine clearing.

Do not try to force out the last of the juice, or again you will cloud the wine. Give it time to run through naturally (this is where the pectic enzyme helps). It pays to be patient here. Stir well to make sure that all sugar is thoroughly dissolved, then pour into fermenting jar and top up with cold water. Fit trap and allow ferment to finish. (It may be slow getting going again after you have used the jelly bag or otherwise strained it thoroughly, but do not worry about this. Enough yeast will pass through to cause a ferment, but you must give it time to multiply again.) Rack when the wine is really clear, and again three months later if a second yeast deposit is thrown. Bottle in dark bottles.

Dandelion Wine

Above all, in spring, do not neglect to make dandelion wine, for it is an excellent accompaniment for fish and poultry, and will not disgrace anyone's table. Three trade secrets: use the right quantity of flowers, make sure the blooms are fully open, and, whatever you do, do not soak them above three days, or the wine will have a foul bouquet.

Ingredients

- 3 quarts (3 liters) flowers
- 2 lb, 11 oz (1.2 kg) sugar
- 2 lemons
- 1 orange
- Yeast
- 5 fl oz (150 ml) grape concentrate or 1 lb (450 g) raisins
- Water to 5 quarts (4.5 liters)

Method

Gather the flowers on a sunny day when they are fully open (traditionally St. George's Day, April 23, is the time) and make your wine the same day, while they are fresh. Pick the heads off the stalks, leaving as little stalk as possible. There is no need to pick off individual petals, as some advocate. Put the blooms into a polythene bucket, and pour 136 fl oz (4 liters) of water, boiling, over them. Leave for three days (this is the absolute maximum, and two will do) stirring each day and keeping the bowl closely covered. Then strain the whole into a boiler and add the sugar and the rinds of the lemon and orange, from which you have extracted the juice. Do not include any white pith. Boil for an hour, then return to the bucket and add the juice of the lemons and orange. Allow to cool to 70°F (20°C), then add a good wine yeast, or a level teaspoon of granulated yeast, and some yeast nutrient, since this is a liquor likely to be deficient in desirable elements. Keep the bucket closely covered for three days in a warm place, then strain into a fermenting jar and add the concentrate or raisins before fitting a fermentation lock. Leave until the wine clears, then rack, through a sieve, into a clean jar and leave until Christmas, by which time this wine is usually fit to drink. Another six months of storage, however (particularly in a cask), will bring a noticeable improvement.

DATE WINE

This is a variation upon one of the old-fashioned recipes, but a good one, despite the variety of ingredients.

INGREDIENTS

- 1 lb (450 g) dates
- ½ lb (225 g) barley
- 1 orange
- 1 lemon
- 2½ lb (1.2 kg) sugar
- ½ nutmeg
- Yeast and nutrient
- Water to 5 quarts (4.5 liters)

METHOD

Chop up the dates and slice the orange and lemon. Boil the barley in 136 fl oz (4 liters) of water for ten minutes, then strain onto the dates and citrus fruit. Add the half nutmeg (it should not be grated). Simmer for twelve minutes, then strain onto the sugar, and stir well to dissolve. Cool to 70°F (20°C), add the yeast and nutrient, and keep in a warm place, closely covered, for five days, stirring daily. Then pour into fermenting jar, top up with cold water, and fit fermentation lock. Leave until it begins to clear, then rack and move into a cooler place. Rack into clean bottles when completely clear and stable.

"There must be an easier way!"

Date and Apricot Wine

Ingredients

- 2 lb (1 kg) dates
- 1 lb (450 g) dried apricots
- ½ lb (225 g) barley (if desired)
- 2 lb, 11 oz (1.2 kg) sugar
- 2 oranges
- 2 lemons
- Yeast and nutrient
- Water to 5 quarts (4.5 liters)

Method

Peel the citrus fruit and chop the dates. Bring 112 fl oz (3.5 liters) of water to the boil. Add the fruit, citrus peel, and barley if used (barley lends body to the wine, but alters the true flavor). Simmer for ten minutes, then strain onto the sugar and juice of the oranges and lemons. Stir well, allow to cool to 70°F (20°C), then pour into fermentation jar and add yeast and nutrient. Fit fermentation lock. Top up with water when ferment slows and ferment right out in the usual way. Rack when it first clears and bottle three months later. A variation is to use 3 lb (1.3 kg) dates and omit the apricots.

"Red or white? It doesn't matter; I'm color blind!"

ELECAMPANE WINE
(Inula Helenium)

"The wine wherein the root of Elecampane hath steept is singular good against colicke."
Markham, Country Farme, 1616

INGREDIENTS

- 1 small packet elecampane herb
- 1 marrow 2-3 lb (1-1.5 kg)
- ½ oz (15 g) citric acid (or 3 lemons, no pith, in lieu)
- 3 lb (1.3 kg) sugar
- A pinch of grape tannin
- Yeast nutrient and activated wine yeast
- Water to 5 quarts (4.5 liters)

METHOD

Pour 112 fl oz (3.5 liters) boiling water over the grated or sliced marrow, including the seeds, and leave this, well covered, to soak for twenty-four hours. Then pour 20 fl oz (570 ml) of boiling water over the elecampane herb and infuse as for tea. Strain over sugar. Add the strained marrow infusion, the citric acid, and tannin, and stir well until all is dissolved. When cool, add the yeast nutrient and activated yeast. Make up to 5 quarts (4.5 liters) when the ferment slows. Ferment under an air lock until it clears, then rack for the first time. Bottle when completely clear (about four months later).

FENNEL WINE
(Foeniculum vulgare)

"It is much used in drink to make people more lean that are too fat."
Culpeper

INGREDIENTS
- 1 small packet fennel herb
- 3 lb (1.3 kg) beetroot
- 2 lb (1.2 kg) sugar
- ½ oz (15 g) citric acid (or 3 lemons, no pith, in lieu)
- 8 fl oz (250 ml) cold strong tea (or a pinch of grape tannin)
- Yeast nutrient and activated wine yeast
- Water to 5 quarts (4.5 liters)

METHOD
Wash the beetroot well and slice thinly, then boil in 112 fl oz (3.5 liters) of water until slightly tender. Strain onto the sugar. Pour 8 fl oz (250 ml) of boiling water over the fennel herb and infuse as for tea. Strain onto sugared beetroot juice. When cool, add the citric acid, cold tea, yeast nutrient, and activated wine yeast. Ferment under an air lock, topping up with cold water when the ferment quiets. Rack for the first time when wine clears. Bottle when completely clear (about three weeks later).

FIG WINE

INGREDIENTS

- 2 lb (1 kg) dried figs
- 2 lb, 11 oz (1.2 kg) sugar
- 1 orange
- 1 lemon
- Water to 5 quarts (4.5 liters)

METHOD

Soak the figs overnight in a little cold water, then make the quantity up to 112 fl oz (3.5 liters). Bring to the boil and simmer for five minutes. Strain onto the sugar, stir well to dissolve, and top up to shoulder of jar. Add the juice of the citrus fruit. When cool, 70°F (20°C), add the yeast and nutrient and ferment under an air lock in the usual way, topping up to bottom of neck with cold water as fermentation slows. It will usually take about three months to clear, when it can be racked, and another two months to be ready for bottling.

"Just a little invention of my own."

Fig and Sultana (Golden Glow)

Ingredients

- 2 lb (1 kg) natural brown sugar*
- 2 lb (1 kg) sultanas
- 2 lb (1 kg) figs
- 8 oz (225 g) barley
- Yeast and nutrient
- Water to 5 quarts (4.5 liters)

Method

This makes a wine of good color and body, and about twelve percent alcohol. Put the barley to soak overnight in 10 fl oz (280 ml) of water. The next day, mince the barley and chop the sultanas and fruit, dropping them into a polythene bucket or crock. Meanwhile, bring 136 fl oz (3.75 liters) of water to the boil. Pour it, boiling, over the grain and fruit, and stir in the sugar. Allow to cool to 70°F (20°C), then add the yeast and yeast nutrient (a sherry or sauternes yeast is excellent, but failing that, use a level teaspoon of granulated yeast). Ferment on the pulp for ten days, stirring once a day. Then strain through a nylon sieve or two thicknesses of muslin into a fermenting jar and fit air lock, topping up to within ¾ in (20 mm) of the bottom of the cork with cold boiled water if necessary. Ferment out and rack when it clears (about eight weeks). Rack again after a further two months or so into clean bottles.

   *Natural brown sugar is made through the partial refinement of sugar cane extract. Adding molasses to fully refined sugar is how most brown sugar is made. Natural brown sugar is generally drier and paler, and has larger crystals than standard brown sugar.

Ginger Wine

Ingredients

- 3 oz (80 g) root ginger
- 2 oranges
- 2 lemons
- ½ lb (225 g) raisins
- 3 lb (1.3 kg) sugar
- Yeast and nutrient
- Water to 5 quarts (4.5 liters)

Method

Peel the fruit thinly, avoiding the white pith, and put the peel and juice of the oranges and lemons into a bucket or bowl with the chopped raisins. Bring 112 fl oz (3.5 liters) of water to the boil and add the sugar and ginger, well crushed. Boil for thirty minutes and make up, if necessary, to about 112 fl oz (3.5 liters). Bring it to the boil again and pour onto the rinds and fruit. Then allow the liquor to cool to 70°F (20°C) (this can be sped up by standing the bucket in cold water after the first ten minutes). Add the yeast and yeast nutrient. Cover and leave in a warm 65°-70°F (17°-20°C) place for ten days or so. Next, strain into a fermenting jar, top up, and fit air lock. Bottle when it clears and fermentation is finished.

Happy birthday, dear.

Ginger Glow

Ingredients

- 2 lb, 11 oz (1.2 kg) sugar
- ½ oz (15 g) essence ginger
- ½ oz (15 g) essence cayenne
- ½ oz (15 g) burnt sugar or 16 fl oz (500 ml) strong tea
- ½ oz (15 g) tartaric acid
- Yeast and nutrient
- Water to 5 quarts (4.5 liters)

Method

Put the sugar in fermenting bucket and add 112 fl oz (3.5 liters) boiling water to dissolve. When cool, add the essences, etc., and introduce yeast and nutrient. Fit lock and ferment in usual way, topping up as necessary with cold water.

Goats-Beard Wine

(Tragopogon-Pratensis)

C. Shave

Found in meadows, the yellow-flowered goats-beard has a folk name "John go to bed at noon" due to the fact that its flowers open at four o'clock in the morning and close by noon. It flowers throughout June and July.

Ingredients

- 5 quarts (4.5 liters) goats-beard flowers
- 3 lb (1.3 kg) sugar
- 1 teaspoon grape tannin
- 2 lemons or ½ oz (15 g) citric acid
- Activated yeast and nutrient
- Water to 5 quarts (4.5 liters)

Method

Remove stalks and put the flowers into a polythene bucket with the grated lemon rinds (no pith) and sugar. Pour on 112 fl oz (3.5 liters) boiling water, stir to dissolve the sugar, and leave to cool. Add cold tea, lemon juice or citric acid, activated yeast, and yeast nutrient. Cover bucket and leave for two days, then strain into fermenting jar, top up to bottom of neck with cold water, and fit air lock. Ferment out and bottle in usual way.

GOLDEN ROD WINE

"True love lies bleeding, with the hearts-at-ease:
And Golden Rods, and tansy running high
That o'er the pale top smiled on passer-by."

John Clare

Most gardens, if they have any at all, have a profusion of blooms of golden rod, and these will make an excellent wine, particularly if it is made not too sweet. It is a glorious golden color.

INGREDIENTS

- 20 fl oz (570 ml) blossom (not pressed down)
- 1¾ lb (850 g) white sugar
- 1½ lb (225 g) raisins
- 6 sweet oranges
- Yeast and nutrient
- Water to 5 quarts (4.5 liters)

METHOD

Bring 112 fl oz (3.5 liters) of water to the boil and dissolve the sugar in it, stirring for a minute or two to ensure that this is complete. Then pour the boiling syrup over the flowers and raisins and add the orange juice. Allow the liquor to cool to 70°F (20°C), then add the yeast and the yeast nutrient. Leave to stand for five days, covered closely, in a temperature of about 65°F (17°C). Give it a good stir from the bottom once or twice daily. Then strain into a jar, filling it to just below the bottom of the neck, and fit a fermentation lock. When the wine has noticeably cleared and there is an appreciable deposit, rack into a clean jar. Repeat the racking three to four months later, this time into bottles. The wine will be at its best about six months later.

GRAPE AND SULTANA

INGREDIENTS

- 1 lb (450 g) sultanas
- 1 lb (450 g) grapes
- 1¾ lb (850 g) sugar
- 8 oz (225 g) barley
- Yeast and nutrient
- Water to 5 quarts (4.5 liters)

METHOD

Soak the barley overnight in half a pint of (extra) water. The next day, mince both grain and sultanas. Bring 112 fl oz (3.5 liters) of water to the boil and pour it over the grain and fruit, then crush the grapes manually and add. Stir in the sugar and make sure that it is all dissolved. Allow to cool until just tepid, 70°F (20°C), then introduce the yeast, preferably a sherry yeast, and nutrient. Ferment, closely covered for ten days, stirring daily. Strain into fermenting jar, top up with a little cold water, fit air lock, and ferment out in the usual way. Rack when clear and bottle after a further two months.

"Do hurry up with the wine, dear, the guests are arriving..."

Greengage Wine

Plums are commonly used for wine, and it is puzzling that greengages are not more popular for the purpose, for they make a wine that many think superior in both taste and appearance to that made from "blue" plums, which often has an unattractive color. Do not neglect to use a pectic enzyme for this wine.

Ingredients

- 4 lb (2 kg) greengages
- 3 lb (1.3 kg) sugar
- Yeast and nutrient
- Pectic enzyme
- Water to 5 quarts (4.5 Iiters)

Method

Cut up the greengages and pour 112 fl oz (3.5 liters) of boiling water over them. Let it cool considerably before adding the pectic enzyme. Keep well covered for four days, mashing the fruit with the hands and stirring it well each day.

Then strain the liquor onto the sugar, add the yeast and nutrient, and transfer to fermentation jar with trap. It is best to use a vigorously fermenting yeast starter and to start the fermentation (for three days at least) at a comparatively high temperature, between 70°-75°F (20°-25°C). Then reduce it to 65°F (17°C) and top up with cold water to bottom of neck. Rack the wine when it clears, and repeat the process two or three months later. This is a clean medium-sweet wine most useful for table purposes.

Hawthorn Berry Wine

Ingredients

* 5 quarts (4.5 liters) hawthorn berries
* 2 lb, 10 oz (1.2 kg) white sugar
* 2 lemons
* Yeast and nutrient
* Water to 5 quarts (4.5 liters)

Method

Wash the berries in a colander under a running tap, then place them in a bowl or crock and bruise them with a stainless steel spoon or piece of hardwood. Pour over them 112 fl oz (3.5 liters) water (cold) and add the juice and thin peel of the lemons, being careful to exclude any white pith, which will give the wine a distinctly bitter taste.

Cover your bucket closely with a folded towel and leave it for five or six days so the flavor can be drawn from the berries. Do not forget to give it a daily stir. Then strain onto the sugar and stir well to dissolve it. Finally, add your yeast and the requisite amount of any yeast nutrient, and stir in well. Pour the yeasted liquor into a fermenting jar, filling it to the shoulder and fitting an air lock. Fit fermentation trap and keep the jar in a warm place 65°-70°F (17°-20°C). After a week or so, the ferment will have quieted and the fermenting jar can then be topped up as full as possible with cold water and the trap refitted. When the wine clears and a good yeast sediment has formed, rack for the first time (this is usually after two and a half to three months). Rack again into bottles two months later. This is a distinctive and agreeable table wine.

Herbal Delight

C. S. Shave

Ingredients

- 2 tablespoons mixed herbs
- ½ oz (225 g) citric acid
- 10 fl oz (280 ml) stewed tea
- 3 lb (1.3 kg) sugar
- 112 fl oz (3.5 liters) water
- Yeast and nutrient

Method

Dissolve 2 lb (1 kg) sugar in 112 fl oz (3.5 liters) of boiling water and pour over the herbs. Add the citric acid and stewed tea. When cool, add yeast and yeast nutrient, and leave to ferment for forty-eight hours in a warm place. Strain. Then top up with the remaining sugar. Fit fermentation lock and ferment to completion. The wine should be racked (i.e., siphoned off the yeast deposit) after about three months.

"I think he found it quite a tonic!"

HUCKLEBERRY WINE

(Solanum nigrum var. Guineense)

INGREDIENTS

- 3 lb (1.3 kg) garden huckleberries
- 2 lb, 11 oz (1.2 kg) sugar
- Yeast and nutrient
- Water to 5 quarts (4.5 liters)

METHOD

Pick the berries when they are fully ripe and crush them in a bowl with a stainless steel spoon. Add 112 fl oz (3.5 liters) of water and mix thoroughly. Allow to stand overnight, then strain through a nylon sieve onto the sugar and stir well to dissolve. Add yeast and nutrient, cover closely with a sheet of polythene or thick cloth, and leave in a warm place, 70°-75°F (17°-20°C), for a week. When first vigorous ferment subsides, stir and transfer to fermenting jar. Fit fermentation lock and place in an area with a temperature of 60°-65°F (15°-17°C) for the main fermentation. Top up with cold water as necessary. If possible, use a colored or opaque jar to keep out the light, or wrap your clear glass jar with brown paper. Rack for first time after three months, refit air lock, and rack again into clean bottles after a further three months.

Kohlrabi Wine

Ingredients

- 4 lb (2 kg) kohlrabi
- 1 orange or ½ oz (15 g) citric acid
- 1 lemon
- 2 lb, 11 oz (1.2 kg) sugar
- Yeast and nutrient

Method

Scrub the roots well (it is not necessary to peel them) and cut them into ¼ in (6 mm) slices. Put them into a large saucepan or boiler in 96 fl oz (3 liters) of water. Bring to the boil and simmer until tender. Do not, however, allow them to go mushy or the wine will not clear. Strain the liquor onto the sliced fruit and sugar. Simmer for half an hour, stirring well for the first few minutes, then strain through a nylon sieve into a fermenting jar and allow to cool to 70°F (20°C) before adding your yeast and nutrient. Plug jar with cotton wool for the first four days until the fermentation quiets, then top up with 16-24 fl oz (500-700 ml) cold water and fit air lock. After a week, move into a slightly lower temperature. After three months, the wine should be clearing and can be racked or siphoned into a clean bottle, leaving the sediment behind. Refit air lock and leave for a further three months, then rack again, this time into wine bottles, and cork securely. The same recipe can be used for turnip wine.

LAVENDER

INGREDIENTS

- 32 fl oz (1 liter) lavender leaves (no stalk)
- 7 fl oz (200 ml) grape concentrate
- 2 lb, 12 oz (1.2 kg) sugar
- ½ oz (15 g) citric acid (or 3 lemons, no pith)
- 8 fl oz (250 ml) cold strong tea or pinch of grape tannin
- Yeast nutrient and activated yeast
- Water to 5 quarts (4.5 liters)

METHOD

Pour 112 fl oz (3.5 liters) of boiling water over the lavender leaves and steep for twenty-four hours. Then strain over the sugar and concentrate and stir until all is dissolved, warming the liquor gently. Cool to 70°F (20°C) and add the tannin or cold tea, acid, yeast, and nutrient. Fit air lock and ferment, rack, and bottle as usual.

LIME FLOWER
C. S. Shave

INGREDIENTS
- 4 full teaspoons lime flower tea
- 1 lb (450 g) chopped raisins
- 2 lb, 12 oz (1.2 kg) sugar
- 2 lemons
- 2 oranges or ½ oz (15 g) citric acid
- Yeast nutrient and yeast
- Water to 5 quarts (4.5 liters)

METHOD
Infuse the tea in 112 fl oz (3.5 liters) boiling water and leave to stand twenty-four hours. Strain and simmer with raisins, grated orange, and lemon peel (no pith). Strain onto sugar and add fruit juices or citric acid. When cool, add yeast nutrient. Introduce activated wine yeast and allow fermentation to proceed (using air lock) in normal way. Rack off the lees when clear.

"Her Ladyship used some of her own gooseberry champagne..."

LOGANBERRY WINE

INGREDIENTS

- 3 lb (1.3 kg) loganberries
- 5 fl oz (150 ml) grape concentrate
- 3 lb (1.3 kg) sugar
- Yeast nutrient
- Pectic enzyme
- Water to 5 quarts (4.5 liters)

METHOD

Wash the fruit in a colander gently so as not to damage it, losing juice. Extract the juice by means of an extractor and add 67 fl oz (2 liters) boiling water, or put fruit in a bucket, pour on boiling water, and mash the berries with a wooden spoon. Add 1 lb (450 g) sugar, stirring well to dissolve. Allow to cool to 70°F (20°C), then introduce the yeast and yeast nutrient. Cover closely and leave for three days, stirring daily. Put the remaining 2 lb (1 kg) sugar in a bowl and strain the fermenting juice onto it. Stir well to dissolve the sugar, then pour into an opaque or dark glass fermenting jar, and fit air lock. Top up if necessary (it should not be). Leave for three months, by which time it should be clearing. Rack off into a clean jar (again a dark one to preserve the color of the wine, which will go tawny if exposed to the light) and top up, if necessary, with boiled water or other red wine. Refit trap. Keep for another three months, then rack off again and bottle in dark bottles. The more fruit you use, the more body it will have, but the bouquet is then likely to be too strong.

MADEIRA-TYPE WINE
P. Duncan and B. Acton

INGREDIENTS
- 3 lb (1.3 kg) plums or greengages
- 20 fl oz (570 ml) white grape concentrate
- 2 lb (1 kg) bananas
- Madeira, or another wine yeast starter, and yeast nutrient
- Tartaric acid and sugar as required
- Pectic enzyme

METHOD
Stone the plums and peel and chop up the bananas (discarding the skins). Combine and mix in the grape concentrate and 1 lb (450 g) sugar. Pour about 100 fl oz (3 liters) boiling water over this mixture. When cool, add the pectic enzyme, yeast nutrient, and actively fermenting yeast starter. Ferment on the pulp for about three to four days, pushing down the cap of pulp at least twice daily, then strain off the fruit, removing as much pulp debris as possible.

Check the acidity and, if necessary, adjust to about 4.5 parts per thousand (in terms of sulfuric acid) by means of tartaric acid (probably ⅓-⅔ oz (9-17 g) according to the ripeness of the plums).

Make a syrup of 2 lb (1 kg) of sugar dissolved in 20 fl oz (570 ml) of water. Add 10 fl oz (280 ml) doses of sugar syrup whenever the gravity drops to 1005 or below. Continue feeding sugar in this way until the yeast reaches its maximum tolerance and fermentation ceases (this may take two to three months). The final volume should then be about 5 quarts (4.5 liters).

After fermentation has ceased, rack the wine and place the jar in an estufa, or hot cupboard, at 90°-130°F (32°-54°C) for three to twelve months according to temperature, racking every three months. Finally, mature the wine at normal temperatures (around 55°F, 13°C) for at least one year, racking at six-month intervals. If a dry Sercial-type wine is required, the adding of sugar dosages should be stopped when the fermentation is causing a gravity drop of only one or two points per day, and providing there is at least fifteen percent alcohol in the wine.

Malmsey-Type Wine

P. Duncan and B. Acton

Ingredients

- 1 lb (450 g) peach pulp
- 4 lb (2 kg) beetroot
- 3 lb (1.3 kg) bananas
- Madeira, or another wine yeast starter, and yeast nutrient
- Pectic enzyme
- Tartaric acid and sugar syrup as required

Method

Wash the beets and cut into hunks. Peel bananas and cut into slices, discarding the skins. Boil the beets and bananas in sufficient water to cover for thirty minutes and strain off the boiling liquor (noting the volume) over the peach pulp plus 2 lb, 11 oz (1.2 kg) sugar. Add enough cold water to make up to 10 quarts (9 liters) approximately. When cool, add the yeast nutrient, pectic enzyme, and actively fermenting yeast starter and ferment on the pulp for two to three days. Strain off the pulp, check acidity, and adjust if necessary as in previous recipe. Continue in the same way, feeding with 10 fl oz (280 ml) doses of syrup and topping up the volume to 15 quarts (13.5 liters) eventually. Makes 15 quarts (13.5 liters).

Mint Wine
C. S. Shave

Ingredients

- 27 fl oz (800 ml) mint leaves (lightly bruised)
- 10 fl oz (280 ml) strong tea
- 3 lb (1.3 kg) sugar
- 2 lemons or citric acid
- Yeast and yeast nutrient
- Water to 5 quarts (4.5 liters)

Method

Dissolve the sugar in 100 fl oz (3 liters) boiling water and pour this over the mint leaves. Add the strong tea, lemon juice or citric acid, and lemon peel (no pith). Cool to 70°F (20°C), then stir in the yeast nutrient and an activated wine yeast, or 1 level teaspoon of granulated yeast. Ferment on the solids for ten days, stirring each day, then strain and place in fermentation jar with fermentation lock, topping up if necessary. Ferment in normal way.

Variations may be made by adding 1 lb (450 g) chopped raisins and reducing sugar by 1 lb (450 g) or by adding 14 fl oz (400 ml) grape concentrate and reducing sugar by 1 lb (450 g).

MULBERRY WINE

INGREDIENTS

- 4 lb (2 kg) mulberries
- 1 lb (450 g) raisins (dried figs, dates, prunes, or apricots may be substituted)
- 2 oz (55 g) dried rose hips/shells (or 2 oz (55 g) dried bananas)
- 2 lb, 11 oz (1.2 kg) sugar
- ½ oz (30 g) citric acid (or 3 lemons, no pith, in lieu)
- A pinch of grape tannin (or 10 fl oz (280 ml) of strong tea)
- Pectic enzyme
- Yeast nutrient and activated wine yeast
- Water to make up 5 quarts (4.5 liters) of must

METHOD

Place the berries, chopped dried fruit, rose hips, and sugar into the initial fermentation vessel. Pour in 100 fl oz (3 liters) boiling water. Macerate and stir well with a stainless steel or wooden spoon to break up the fruits and to dissolve the sugar. When cool, add the citric acid, strong tea, pectic enzyme, and yeast nutrient. Introduce the activated wine yeast and ferment on the pulp for ten days, stirring the must twice daily and keeping it closely covered. For secondary fermentation, strain into fermentation vessel, top up with cold water, and fit air lock. Leave to ferment in the normal way, racking as necessary in due course.

"Not when you're wearing that old lace pinny—I've seen the play!"

Oak Bud Wine

Ingredients

- ½ lb (225 g) oak buds and young leaves
- ½ lb (225 g) dates
- ½ lb (225 g) raisins
- 2 lb (1 kg) sugar
- 1 lemon
- Yeast and nutrient
- Water to 5 quarts (4.5 liters)

Method

Gather the buds and new leaves as soon as the first leaves open. Bring 112 fl oz (3.5 liters) of water to the boil, then add the leaves, buds, chopped dates, and raisins. Simmer for twenty minutes. Strain the liquor onto the sugar and stir well to dissolve. Allow to cool to 70°F (20°C), then add the juice of the lemon, the yeast, and the yeast nutrient. Cover closely and ferment in a warm place for four days before transferring to fermenting jar and fitting air lock. This is an excellent wine for blending purposes, for it will add zest to an insipid wine. If a sweet wine is required, increase the sugar to 2 lb, 11 oz (1.2 kg).

"But it's just full of vitamin C."

OAK LEAF WINE

Young leaves will give a different flavor from those picked later in the year when they are brown-tinted, so here, really, are two wines.

INGREDIENTS

- 136 fl oz (4 liters) oak leaves
- 3 lb (1.3 kg) sugar
- 2 oranges
- 1 lemon
- Yeast and nutrient
- Water to 5 quarts (4.5 liters)

METHOD

Rinse the leaves in clean cold water, then place them in a polythene bucket and pour over them 112 fl oz (3.5 liters) of boiling water. Leave the leaves to steep for twenty-four hours, then strain the liquid into a boiler large enough to take both it and the sugar, with a little room to spare. Add the sugar, the juice of the fruit, and the grated peel, being careful to include no bitter white pith. Bring the whole to the boil and keep it simmering for twenty minutes. This serves the triple purpose of extracting the flavors and essences from the fruit skins, thoroughly dissolving the sugar, and sterilizing the liquor. Allow to cool, strain again through a large nylon sieve or muslin, and when temperature has dropped to 70°F (20°C), add your chosen wine yeast or 1 level teaspoon of granulated yeast. Pour into fermenting jar and fit trap. This wine usually works vigorously and will certainly do so if you include the yeast nutrient. You should have a little headspace in the fermenting bottle for the first four or five days, but after that, top up with cold water when the first vigor of the ferment has subsided. Otherwise, it may foam out through the trap. When the wine has cleared (usually about two to three months), siphon off the yeast sediment and keep for at least six months before use.

Walnut leaf wine can be made in the same way.

Onion Wine

Ingredients

- ½ lb (225 g) onions
- ½ lb (225 g) potatoes
- 1 lb (450 g) chopped raisins
- 2 lb (1 kg) sugar
- 2 lemons or citric acid
- Yeast nutrient and yeast
- Water to 5 quarts (4.5 liters)

Method

Slice and dice the onions and potatoes and place these together with the chopped raisins in 112 fl oz (3.5 liters) of warm (not hot) water in which the sugar has been dissolved. Add lemon juice (no pith) or citric acid and yeast nutrient, then introduce activated yeast. Ferment for ten days, then strain and complete fermentation in glass jars under fermentation lock.

ORANGE AND WHEAT

INGREDIENTS

- 6 Jaffa oranges
- 1 lb (450 g) wheat
- ¼ lb (100 g) raisins
- 1 lemon
- 2 lb, 11 oz (1.2 kg) sugar
- Yeast and nutrient
- Water to 5 quarts (4.5 liters)

METHOD

Bring 112 fl oz (3.5 liters) of water to the boil, then simmer the skins of the citrus fruit in it for a quarter of an hour. Take out the peel and pour the liquid over the sugar, the juice of the oranges and lemons, the washed wheat, and the chopped raisins. Allow to cool to 70°F (20°C) before adding the yeast and yeast nutrient. Keep well covered in a warm place, stirring daily, for ten days. Then strain into fermenting jar and top up if necessary (the grain absorbs some of the liquid). Fit trap and ferment out. Rack and bottle in the usual way.

"Anyone seen my hydrometer?"

Seville Orange Wine

Ingredients

- 6 Seville oranges
- 6 sweet oranges
- 2 lb, 4 oz (1 kg) sugar (for a dry wine)
- 2 lb, 11 oz (1.2 kg) sugar (for a sweet wine)
- Yeast and nutrient
- Water to 5 quarts (4.5 liters)

Method

Wash the oranges in warm water to remove any wax. Peel three of each, keeping the peel thin and avoiding the pith, which imparts a very bitter flavor. Boil 96 fl oz (3 liters) of water and then add the peel to it. Cover and allow to stand for twenty-four hours to extract the zest. Then strain the infusion into a polythene bucket containing the sugar and the juice of all twelve oranges. Stir until all the sugar is dissolved, then add the yeast and yeast nutrient. Cover the bucket closely and stand in a warm place 70°F (20°C) for four or five days, after which the ferment will have quieted a little and the liquor can be poured into a fermenting jar and a trap fitted. Leave until it clears, then rack and bottle as usual.

SWEET ORANGE WINE

INGREDIENTS

- 12 sweet oranges
- 1 lemon
- 3 lb (1.3 kg) sugar
- 1 lb (450 g) large raisins
- Yeast and nutrient
- Water to 5 quarts (4.5 liters)

METHOD

Peel half the oranges and put the skins in the oven, baking them until they are browned. Then pour over them 1 quart (1 liter) of water, boiling. Peel the remaining oranges, and then pulp all the oranges in a polythene bucket. Add the chopped or minced raisins and the Campden tablet. Pour over the fruit 2.5 quarts (2 liters) of water, cold, and the liquid from the orange peel infusion. Stir well, cover closely, and leave for twenty-four hours. Add the lemon juice, yeast, nutrient, and 1 lb (450 g) sugar, stirring well to dissolve. Stir the must daily and keep in a warm place 70°F (20°C). After four days, strain onto remaining sugar, stirring well to dissolve, and pour into fermenting jar. Fit trap and ferment at roughly 65°F (17°C) until clear, then rack. Keep a further two months under air lock before bottling.

"Heavenly bouquet."

PARSLEY AND RICE

Humfrey Wakefield

INGREDIENTS

- ½ lb (225 g) raisins
- 1 quart (1 liter) measure parsley (packed tight)
- ¼ lb (100 g) rice
- 2-2¼ lb (1 kg) sugar
- Grated rind of 2 oranges
- Grated rind and juice of 1 lemon
- Wine yeast and nutrient
- Pectic enzyme, as instructed

METHOD

Boil parsley (well washed) in 2.5 quarts (2 liters) of water. Put in rice and simmer further five minutes. Strain through coarse sieve onto sugar, grated rinds, lemon juice, and coarsely chopped raisins. Stir well. When cool, add yeast (previously propagated in a starter bottle) and the pectic enzyme, dissolved in a little warm water.

Add water (about 2.5 quarts, 2 liters) to bring bulk of must up to near 5 quarts (4.5 liters). Ferment on raisin pulp for two to four days, stirring frequently, and keeping covered. Strain off into 5-quart (4.5 liter) jar through coarse sieve and top up (if necessary) with water. Fit lock. Rack when wine begins to clear and again when fermentation is quite finished.

Produces a light fragrant white table wine, something between pineapple and apricot. Don't worry about chicken broth smell in early stages. It ferments out. If sweet dessert wine is wanted (also good), add a further 1 lb (450 g) sugar when fermentation begins to slow.

PARSNIP WINE

INGREDIENTS

* 4 lb (2 kg) parsnips
* 2 lb, 11 oz (1.2 kg) sugar
* 5 fl oz (150 ml) grape concentrate
* ½ oz (15 g) citric acid
* Pectic emzyme, as directed
* Water to 5 quarts (4.5 liters)

METHOD

Scrub the parsnips and scrape them quickly with a strong knife. Then slice them and boil them in 112 fl oz (3.5 liters) of water until just tender, but on no account so long that they go mushy, or the wine will not clear. If the roots are boiled in half the water, for convenience sake, the remainder can be added later.

Strain through a large nylon sieve onto the remaining water (cold), but do not press the parsnips or hurry the process unduly, or again, the wine may not clear. Add the sugar and concentrate, bring to the boil, and then turn down the heat and simmer gently for three-quarters of an hour. Turn into a crock or pan and allow to cool to 70°F (20°C). Then add pectic enzyme, citric acid, yeast, and yeast nutrient (preferably a wine yeast, but a level teaspoon of granulated yeast can be employed failing anything better). Cover closely with a thick cloth and keep in a warm place, 60°-70°F (17°-20°C), for a week. Then pour into fermenting jar, top up, and fit air lock. Rack when it clears and re-fit air lock. Rack for the second time after a further three months.

Parsnip Wine (Spiced)

Ingredients

- 6 lb (3 kg) parsnips
- 2 lb, 11 oz (1.2 kg) sugar
- 1 lemon
- 2 oranges
- 1 oz (30 g) root ginger
- Yeast and yeast nutrient
- Pectic enzyme
- Water to 5 quarts (4.5 liters)

Method

Midwinter is the time to make this wine, for the sugar content of the roots will have been concentrated by the winter frosts. Scrape or scrub the parsnips clean (a large strong-bladed knife is a great help), slice them, and boil in 112 fl oz (3.5 liters) of water until tender, but not mushy. (Be careful not to overdo the boiling or you will subsequently have difficulty clearing the wine. If you have a press, you need boil for only five to ten minutes, for you can then press the parsnips afterwards.) The bruised ginger and the thinly-pared rinds of the citrus fruit are boiled in with the parsnips (or separately, in a quart (liter) or so of the water if you are using the press. This is then added to the remainder). Strain all the liquid onto the juice of the fruit and dissolve the sugar in it, stirring well. Cool to 70°F (20°C), then add the yeast, yeast nutrient, and pectic enzyme. Cover. Stir daily. Four or five days later, stir, pour into fermenting jar, and fit trap. Leave in a warm place to ferment until the wine clears and a yeast deposit has formed (about two months). Then rack for the first time. Refit trap and leave until completely clear and stable (another two months or so), then rack again and bottle.

PARSNIP AND FIG

INGREDIENTS

- 3 lb (1.3 kg) parsnips
- 1 lb (450 g) dried figs
- ½ lb (225 g) raisins
- ½ lb (225 g) rice
- 2 lb, 11 oz (1.2 kg) sugar
- Yeast and yeast nutrient
- Pectic enzyme
- Water to 5 quarts (4.5 liters)

METHOD

Scrub or scrape the parsnips, slice them, and boil them in half the water with the chopped figs and raisins until only just tender (usually not more than twenty minutes). Do not overcook so that the parsnips go soft and mushy, or the wine may subsequently be difficult to clear. Strain the liquor onto the rice, bring to the boil, and boil for four minutes. Strain onto the sugar and stir well to dissolve. Allow the liquor to cool to 70°F (20°C). Then add the pectic enzyme, yeast (a sherry yeast is excellent), and yeast nutrient, and pour into a fermenting jar or bottle. Fill to shoulder adding cold boiled water if necessary, and fit an air lock. After about a week in a temperature of 65°-70°F (17°-20°C), the first vigorous ferment will have subsided and the jar can be topped up to the bottom of the neck. When the wine begins to clear and a yeast deposit has formed (six weeks to two months), siphon it off the lees into a fresh bottle and refit lock. Leave for a further three months before bottling. This will usually produce a dry wine if a good nutrient has been used. Some readers may care to add 4-8 oz (120-225 g) more sugar either before fermentation ceases or to the finished wine.

Peach Perfection

This is a recipe by Mrs. Cherry Leeds of Thames Ditton for a peach wine that is so superb and inexpensive that we give the fullest possible instructions. It sounds extravagant, but it is not. Keep an eye out at the grocery store, and you will see that in August (usually about the first two weeks) peaches tend to come down in price. Mrs. Leeds uses a Kitzinger sherry or Tokay yeast for this recipe.

To Make 50 Quarts (45 liters)

Ingredients

- 30 lb (13 kg) peaches
- 32 lb (14 kg) natural brown sugar
- Boiling and boiled water
- 3 oz (85 g) citric acid
- 1½ teaspoons tannin
- 3 oz (85 g) pectic enzyme

Method

Wipe peaches and remove the stones. Drop into large container such as a polythene bin. Scrub hands well and squeeze the peaches until well mashed. Cover well with boiling water and leave covered overnight.

The next day, stir in the pectic enzyme and cover well. On the third day, strain through a sieve or muslin, twice if possible, to reduce sludge and put into the 50-quart (45 liter) jar. Add citric acid, tannin, and nutrient.

At this point, it is a simple matter to place the jar or carboy into the position it will occupy during fermentation. Put 20 lb (9 kg) of sugar into the large container, add sufficient boiling water to dissolve it, and add to the jar when cool. Bring the level of the liquid up to the turn of the shoulder of the jar with boiled water. Open the yeast sachet or packet, pour in, and fit fermentation lock. The gravity at this stage will be about 1100 (the original gravity is almost invariably 1025-1030). Fermentation will start on the third day if the temperature is sufficient: 70°-75°F (20°-25°C).

The rest of the sugar is added in stages from now on. Make the first addition of 2.5 quarts (2 liters) of syrup when the gravity is 1030 (roughly after two weeks). The sugar is then added in 1 quart (1 liter) lots when the gravity is between 1010 and 1015 each time. The syrup used is 2.2 lb (1 kg) sugar to 10 fl oz (570 ml) boiling water and cooled, thus making 1 quart (1 liter) syrup.

The fermenting period lasts for about seven or eight months, though one can keep it going for a year with small additions of syrup.

The first racking takes place when all the sugar is in and the reading is 1010. Some of the wine will have to be removed to accommodate the last 1 quart (1 liter) of syrup. Stir up the jar and remove about a liter. Put it aside under an air lock and use it to top up the jar after the first racking. Stir the liquid vigorously with an oak rod once a day for the first few weeks.

Because of the pectic enzyme used, the wine will clear perfectly and after the first racking will become crystal clear, but don't be tempted to rack again until fermentation has ceased finally. This usually happens when the gravity is about 1005.

The alcoholic content will be about eighteen percent.

To Make 25 Quarts (22.5 liters)

For 25-quart (22.5 liter) jars, use half quantities except for the pectic enzyme. Use 2 oz (55 g) for the pectic enzyme, otherwise the procedure is the same.

To Make 5 Quarts (4.5 liters)

INGREDIENTS
- 3 lb (1.3 kg) peaches
- 1 teaspoon citric acid
- ½ oz (15 g) pectic enzyme
- Spoonful tannin
- 2 lb (1 kg) sugar
- 2.5 quarts (2 liters) boiling water

METHOD
The method is the same, but the yeast starter bottle should be prepared on the same day as mashing, and the sugar is put in all together, just before the yeast starter.

Plum Wine

Ingredients

- 4 lb (2 kg) plums
- 3 lb (1.3 kg) white sugar
- Yeast and yeast nutrient
- Pectic enzyme
- Water to 5 quarts (4.5 liters)

Method

Wash the fruit and cut it up, then put it in a bowl and pour over it 96 fl oz (3 liters) of water, boiling. Cover it with a thick cloth or sheet of polythene. When it is cool, add the pectic enzyme according to maker's instructions. Leave four days, giving it an occasional stir. Then strain through a nylon sieve or muslin. Dissolve sugar in the juice and add yeast. Cover again. Two days later, pour into fermenting jar and fit trap. Top up to the bottom of the neck with cold water. When the wine clears, siphon off the lees. Keep for a further three months, then rack into bottles. More fruit can be used if available to lend more body to the wine, or 1 lb (450 g) of wheat or barley (plum wine does tend to be rather thin).

"So much for encouraging junior to take up a hobby."

Plum Wine

Ingredients

- 4 lb (2 kg) plums
- 1 lemon
- 2 lb, 11 oz (1.2 kg) sugar
- 4 cloves
- ½ oz (15 g) root ginger
- Yeast and nutrient
- Pectic enzyme
- Water to 5 quarts (4.5 liters)

Method

This is basically an old recipe from a time when additional flavorings were favored. The recipe is just as successful when the cloves and ginger are omitted.

Cut up the plums, remove the stones, and add to them the crushed ginger, the cloves, and the sliced lemon. Bring 3 quarts (3 liters) of water to the boil, pour it over these ingredients, and stir. When it cools, add the pectic enzyme. Cover and leave for three or four days, stirring twice daily. Strain through a fine sieve onto the sugar, stir to dissolve it, and add the yeast and nutrient. Put into fermenting jar, top up with water to bottom of neck, and fit trap. Leave to ferment to a finish in a warm place. When clear and stable, siphon off into clean bottles and cork.

Cherry Plum Wine

Mrs. Dorothy Cuthbertson, Liverpool Guild

Ingredients

- 4 lb (2 kg) cherry plums
- 1 lb (450 g) raisins (chopped)
- 2 teaspoons citric acid
- 2 lb, 11 oz (1.2 kg) sugar (according to taste)
- ¼ teacup of strong tea
- All-purpose wine yeast and nutrient
- Pectic enzyme

Method

Wash fruit. Cover with 96 fl oz (3 liters) boiling water. Add 2 lb (1 kg) sugar, tea, raisins, and citric acid. When cool, add pectic enzyme, yeast starter, and yeast food. Stir and squeeze the fruit daily for five days, then strain into fermentation jar and fit lock. Add sugar in syrup form as required. (Not more than 1 lb (450 g) dissolved in 8 fl oz (250 ml) of water.)

Keep the fermentation going as long as possible, but when it finally ceases and the wine is clear and stable, siphon into clean bottles.

PORT-TYPE WINE
P. Duncan and B. Acton

INGREDIENTS

- 3 lb (1.3 kg) elderberries
- 2 lb (1 kg) bananas
- 20 fl oz (570 ml) red grape concentrate
- Tartaric acid, nutrient, sugar syrup as required
- Port yeast or wine yeast of choice

METHOD

Mash elderberries to extract juice and leach pulp with 20 fl oz (570 ml) cold water. Boil bananas in 1 quart (1 liter) water and add liquor to elderberry juice, plus leachings and grape concentrate. Bring volume up to 136 fl oz (4 liters) and adjust acid to between 3.5 and 4.0 parts per thousand as sulfuric acid (this requires the addition of ½ oz (15 g) tartaric acid). Add yeast nutrient and a good port yeast culture when cool. Feed with additions of syrup in 5 fl oz (150 ml) lots (syrup made with 2 lb (1 kg) sugar in 20 fl oz (570 ml) of water) whenever the wine tastes dry or drops in gravity to 1005. When fermentation is almost finished, rack and top up to 5 quarts (4.5 liters) with water and syrup so that the final gravity is around 1010.

In view of the relatively high cost of this wine, it will be worth keeping for at least two years, preferably three, racking at three-month intervals so that the maximum flavor and smoothness may develop.

An equally satisfactory port-type wine can be made by using 3 lb (1.3 kg) blackberries, 2 lb (1 kg) sloes or damsons, and 1 lb (450 g) elderberries. Mash and leach the elderberries, then proceed as above.

For a tawny wine, use 6 lb (3 kg) blackberries only and keep finished wine for three or four years.

Prune Wine

H. E. Bravery

Ingredients

- 4 lb (2 kg) prunes
- 2 lemons
- 2 lb, 11 oz (1.2 kg) sugar
- Yeast and nutrient
- Pectic enzyme
- Water to 5 quarts (4.5 liters)

Method

Wash the prunes in water and put them in the fermenting vessel. Boil 1¾ lb (800 g) of sugar in 96 fl oz (3 liters) of water and pour over the fruit while boiling. Allow to cool and add the yeast and pectic enzyme. Cover and ferment for ten days, crushing well each day as soon as the fruit has become soft.

After ten days, crush well and strain out the solids. Wring out as dry as you can and put the strained liquor into a 5-quart (4.5 liter) jar.

Boil the remaining 14 oz (400 g) of sugar in 10 fl oz (280 ml) of water and add to the rest when cool. Top up with a little cold water if necessary. Cover or fit fermentation lock and leave until all fermentation has ceased. Then rack and bottle as usual.

"We hate small glasses."

Prune and Wheat Wine
Syd Lowe

Ingredients

- 1 lb (450 g) prunes (best quality)
- 1 lb (450 g) wheat (best quality)
- ¼ lb (100 g) raisins
- 2.2 lb (1 kg) sugar
- 1 yeast nutrient tablet
- Pectic enzyme
- 2 Vitamin B tablets (Aneurine hydrochloride BP)
- Yeast, sherry yeast (or 1 level teaspoon dried yeast)
- Water to 5 quarts (4.5 liters)

Method

Cut each prune through with a knife and place in a bucket. Place wheat in a moderate oven to lightly bake (do not allow to brown over), then add to prunes. Add yeast nutrient, raisins, pectic enzyme (as makers direct), and Vitamin B. Pour on 112 fl oz (3.5 liters) of water that has been boiled and allowed to cool. Cover and stir very thoroughly every day for ten days. Strain and press pulp to extract all the juice. (Do this with your hands if no other means are available.) Add 1¾ lb (800 g) sugar made into syrup with a small amount of warm water. Add yeast and stir thoroughly to mix.

Leave this in a warm place for about ten days, then strain through muslin or jelly bag into a 5-quart (4.5 liter) jar and fit air lock. After it has been in the jar for about ten days, sample and, if necessary, add a little of the remaining 1 lb (450 g) of sugar. Repeat this after another ten days, then add the balance. Top up with cold water if necessary.

Leave until fermentation is complete. Strain into a clean jar, fit cork, and leave in cool place until clear (a cellar is ideal). Bottle.

PUMPKIN WINE

INGREDIENTS

- 4 lb (2 kg) pumpkin
- 2 lb, 11 oz (1.2 kg) white sugar
- 2 lemons
- 1 oz (55 g) root ginger (this can be omitted if desired)
- 2 oranges
- Yeast and nutrient
- Water to 5 quarts (4.5 Iiters)

METHOD

Grate the pumpkin, slice the oranges and lemons, bruise the ginger, and put them all into a polythene bucket. Pour over them 112 fl oz (3.5 liters) of boiling water. Add the yeast and nutrient when cool. Allow to stand for five days closely covered, stirring frequently, then strain. Dissolve the sugar in the liquid. After four or five days of fermentation, closely covered, put it into a fermentation jar and fit trap. When it clears, siphon off the yeast. The wine should be ready after about six months and can then be bottled.

"Grape? Haven't you got any PROPER wine?"

RED CURRANT WINE

This is a popular wine and well worth making, but it often tends to turn out disappointingly thin for those who prefer good body in their wines. If you require a delicate wine, make it according to the recipe, but if you want a slightly heavier wine, use additional fruit, about ½ lb (225 g) of rolled barley, and pour the water on boiling instead of cold. Also omit the pectic enzyme and Campden tablet.

INGREDIENTS

- 3 lb (1.3 kg) red currants
- 3 lb (1.3 kg) sugar
- Pectic enzyme
- Yeast and nutrient
- Water to 5 quarts (4.5 liters)

METHOD

Put the fruit in a polythene bucket and crush thoroughly. Add 2.5 quarts (2 liters) of cold water and one crushed Campden tablet. Twenty-four hours later, add the pectic enzyme according to the instructions. Cover closely and leave for five or six days, stirring daily. Strain through a nylon sieve or jelly bag, expressing as much juice as possible into a fermenting vessel. Add the sugar, stirring well to dissolve. Add the yeast and nutrient, fit a fermentation lock, and leave in a temperature of about 70°F (20°C) to ferment. Top up a week later, if necessary, with cold water. Rack the wine off the lees when it clears, refit the air lock, and repeat the process about three months later, when it will probably be stable and ready to bottle. Again, dark bottles will preserve its delicate color.

RED CURRANT WINE

INGREDIENTS

- 4 lb (2 kg) red currants
- 136 fl oz (4 liters) water
- 3½ lb (1.6 kg) sugar
- Yeast and nutrient

METHOD

As for cherry (first recipe, page 41) or black currant (page 32).

About Oxalic Acid

Many older winemaking books lay undue emphasis upon the presence of oxalic acid in rhubarb because the acid is poisonous. The oxalic acid, however, is contained in the leaves of the plant, not in the stalks that we winemakers use.

Rhubarb is unduly acidic, however, and it may well be advisable to reduce the natural acid a little and/or to use some citric acid in a recipe.

Acid can be removed before fermentation by stirring in 1 oz per 5 quarts (30 g per 4.5 liters) of precipitated chalk or powdered cuttlefish. The juice will effervesce. If afterwards it still has an acid taste, add up to another ½ oz (15 g), but not more. Finally, to give you the acidity you need, add the juice of three lemons or 1 heaping teaspoon of citric acid. A little more may be necessary. Taste the juice and adjust to taste or test with a titration kit.

RHUBARB GOLDEN DREAM

INGREDIENTS

- 6 lb (3 kg) red rhubarb
- 1 lb (450 g) malt extract
- 4 lb (2 kg) white sugar
- Pinch of grape tannin
- 2 lemons (or 1 teaspoon citric acid)
- Yeast

METHOD

Whether or not any acid should be removed by precipitated chalk is a matter of opinion. I have made it with or without. The rhubarb stalks should be picked in mid-May. The malt extract is used to add body to the wine.

Do not peel the rhubarb, but wipe the stalks clean, cut into small short lengths, and cover with cold or warm (not boiling) water. Soak for three days, crushing the rhubarb with the hands after the second day. Strain off into fermenting vessel. Dissolve sugar and malt extract, adding this to the strained rhubarb juice with the tannin and lemon juice, or 1 teaspoon of citric acid. Add yeast nutrient and an activated wine yeast and ferment in the normal way.

"I don't think it really matters HOW you serve wine, do you?"

Rhubarb Memorable Nectar

Ingredients

- 6 lb (3 kg) red rhubarb, picked mid-May
- 1 lb (450 g) raisins
- 10 fl oz (280 ml) strong tea or a little grape tannin
- Yeast nutrient and yeast
- 3½ lb (1.6 kg) sugar
- 2 lemons or 1 teaspoon citric acid

Method

Prepare rhubarb juice as in Golden Dream (page 95). The raisins should be cut up and simmered in the strong tea and the pulp strained into the rhubarb juice. After dissolving the sugar and adding the lemon juice and/or citric acid to the juice, add the yeast nutrient and a working wine yeast. Ferment in the normal way.

RHUBARB GOLDEN PIPKIN

C. Shave

INGREDIENTS

- 3 lb (1.3 kg) red rhubarb
- 7 fl oz (200 ml) strong tea
- 2 lb, 11 oz (1.2 kg) sugar
- 7 fl oz (200 ml) grape concentrate (white)
- 2 lemons or 1 teaspoon citric acid
- Yeast nutrient and yeast

METHOD

Prepare as in Golden Dream (page 95), substituting the grape concentrate for the malt extract. This gives a much lighter and finer wine.

"Rail crash? No, just the Winemakers' Circle committee meeting..."

Christmas Port

Make either Golden Dream (page 95) or Memorable Nectar (page 96) in May and give it its first racking. Blackberries should now be in season.

Pick 3 lb (1.3 kg) blackberries and cover them with 20 fl oz (570 ml) boiling water. Add ¼ lb (110 g) sugar, then squeeze pulp through muslin and add the juice to the racked rhubarb wine. Fit fermentation lock and ferment on in the usual way.

Winter Cheer

Ingredients

- 6 lb (3 kg) red rhubarb (picked mid-May)
- 1 quart (1 liter) balm leaves or 1 packet dried leaves
- 4 lb (2 kg) sugar
- 2 lemons or 1 teaspoon citric acid
- Yeast nutrient and yeast
- 10 fl oz (250 ml) strong tea, or ⅛ teaspoon grape tannin

Method

Prepare rhubarb juice as in Golden Dream (page 95). Put balm leaves in saucepan with water and bring to boil with lemon peel (no pith), cutting off heat as soon as water is boiling. Allow to stand for fifteen minutes. Strain and add this to rhubarb juice, pouring over dissolved sugar, lemon juice or citric acid, and strong tea. Add yeast nutrient and a selected wine yeast and start fermenting in normal way.

Winter Cheer may be varied by the addition of 1 lb (450 g) of malt extract to each 5 quarts (4.5 liters), giving more body, or 1 lb (450 g) of raisins for a mellow flavor.

Rice Wine

(Wheat or rye can be substituted if desired)

Ingredients

- 8 oz (225 g) rice (wheat, rye)
- 6 lb (3 kg) sugar
- 10 quarts (9 liters) water
- ¼ oz (10 g) citric acid
- 1 package sherry yeast
- 1 package nutrient salt
- 1 Campden tablet
- Water to 10 quarts (9 liters)

Method

Two or three days in advance, prepare a starter for the yeast by bringing 20 fl oz (570 ml) apple juice to the boil with a pinch of nutrient salt and 2 tablespoons of sugar. Add yeast and leave, plugged with cotton wool, in a temperature of 70°F (20°C).

On the third day after starting the yeast, boil 8 oz (225 g) rice in 96 fl oz (3 liters) water with 4 tablespoons of sugar for five minutes. Allow to cool. Add the yeast starter, now in full ferment, 1 teaspoon nutrient salt, and citric acid (about 3 level teaspoons).

By the next day, the rice pulp is in vigorous fermentation. Add what remains of the sugar, 6 lb (3 kg) less 6 tablespoons, dissolved in the rest of the water, 10 quarts (9 liters) less 96 fl oz (3 liters). Pour into a clean fermenting jar. Strain the fermenting pulp (when cool) through a clean linen bag or handkerchief onto the syrup with the help of a funnel. Press out lightly with the hands, so that some of the rice starch goes into the jar.

Don't fill to the brim yet, but leave room for foaming. If need be, keep back some of the syrup till the tumultuous ferment has died down (about fourteen days).

The wine will take about two months to ferment right out. Then is the time for the first racking. Top up with pure water and allow a further four weeks in a warm area for the secondary fermentation. Rack again, lightly sulfate with the Campden tablet, and put in a cool area for another four weeks.

The wine will then be as clear as water and can be colored lightly with edible coloring matter or black currant juice before drawing off into bottles. Makes 12.5 quarts (11 liters).

Rice Wine

(Chinese)

Ingredients

- 3 lb (1.3 kg) paddy rice (polished rice will not work)
- 3 lb (1.3 kg) honey
- 5 quarts (4.5 liters) water
- The juice of 2 lemons, 2 oranges

Method

Steep the grain for twenty days in water, stirring every day and keeping well covered. Bring it to the boil and boil it gently until the grains are soft and pulpy. Put it into an earthenware crock with the 5 quarts (4.5 liters) of water. Add various fruits and flowers to the must as desired, along with some honey to give strength, aroma, and color to the wine.

In China, lemon or lime flowers or the juice of oranges or lemons and their thinly peeled rinds are added according to the taste of the maker.

When the must is all well blended and has cooled, yeast is added and it is allowed to ferment in a jar for several days. The wine is then strained into clean glazed vessels, where it clears itself by a second ferment. When the ferment in the second jar is finished, the wine is drawn off into small earthenware jars, which are sealed down and set aside to mature. Well made, this wine is very strong in alcohol content and will keep for many years.

"Just a shade too effervescent!"

RICE WINE
(Old English version)

Steep 3 lb (1.3 kg) of paddy rice in 2.5 quarts (2 liters) of water for six days, stirring every day. Put 3 lb (1.3 kg) of sugar, the juice and rind of two or three lemons and oranges, and, if desired, a few spices into another bowl. Pour 5 quarts (4.5 liters) of boiling water onto the fruit and sugar and stir until it is all blended. Then strain the water from the rice and add it to the mixture. When the liquor has cooled to about 70°F (20°C), add yeast, cover the bowl, and leave for twenty-four hours. Strain carefully into a cask and leave in a warm place to finish the ferment. Top up each morning with water and drop in a stoned raisin each day when the fermentation begins to flag. When all movement has ceased, bung down the cask and store for a year.

ROSE HIP WINE

INGREDIENTS
- 3 lb (1.3 kg) rose hips
- 2.2 lb (1 kg) white sugar
- Yeast and yeast nutrient
- Water to 5 quarts (4.5 liters)

METHOD
Wash the rose hips thoroughly in a colander, then cut them in half or crush them with a piece of wood. A good way of tackling this rather tricky job is to use a domestic mincer with the outer cutting disc removed. Instead, use the fixed disc with the largest holes. This will neatly crush the pips. Put the crushed rose hips and sugar into a crock or polythene trashcan and pour over them 112 fl oz (3.5 liters) of boiling water. Stir well until the sugar is completely dissolved.

Allow the liquor to cool to about 70°F, 20°C (cool enough for you to be able to put your finger in it comfortably). Add yeast (an all-purpose wine yeast or, failing that, a level teaspoon of granulated yeast) together with some yeast nutrient. Cover the container closely with a thick cloth or polythene and leave in a warm place for two weeks, stirring daily.

Strain through a nylon sieve or two thicknesses of butter muslin into a fermentation jar and fit an air lock. This wine usually ferments very vigorously and will normally clear after about three months. Siphon it into a fresh jar, not disturbing the sediment, and leave for a further three months before bottling.

Rose Hip (Dried)

Dried rose hips can be purchased, eliminating the tedious business of picking fresh hips. The dried ones make a wine fully as good, and rose hip wine is good. The Germans hold that the rose hip is second only to the grape for winemaking. With the dried rose hips, which have been largely dehydrated, and therefore weigh less, a smaller quantity is required than when one uses the fresh fruit.

Ingredients

* 10.5 oz (300 g) dried rose hips
* 2.2 lb (1 kg) sugar
* Juice of 1 lemon
* Wine yeast and yeast nutrient
* Water to 5 quarts (4.5 liters)

Method

Prepare your yeast starter two days before making the wine and soak the rose hips overnight in 16 fl oz (500 ml) of water.

Mince your rose hips with an ordinary domestic mincer with the outer cutting disc removed. Put into a bowl with the sugar and lemon juice. Pour over them 96 fl oz (3 liters) of boiling water. Stir well to dissolve the sugar. When the mixture has cooled to 70°F (20°C), add your fermenting yeast. Cover closely with a polythene sheet secured by elastic and stand in a warm place 70°F (20°C). Stir daily. After ten days, strain into a 5-quart (4.5 liter) jar, topping up with cold boiled water to the bottom of the neck if necessary. Fit fermentation lock. When the wine clears, rack into a clean jar and refit lock. Leave for a further three months, then rack into clean bottles and cork down.

ROSE HIP SHELL AND FIG

INGREDIENTS

- 5 oz (150 g) dried rose hip shells
- 3 oz (100 g) dried figs
- 2 lb, 11 oz (1.2 kg) sugar (2.2 lb (1 kg) for a dry wine)
- Wine yeast

METHOD

Put the figs in just enough water to cover them and leave overnight. The next day, add a little more water, bring to the boil, and simmer for ten minutes. Strain the juice into a saucepan and make quantity up to 112 fl oz (3.5 liters). Bring to the boil and pour over the rose hip shells, sugar, and lemon juice. Stir well to dissolve sugar. Allow to cool to 70°F (20°C), then add your yeast. Cover closely with a polythene sheet secured by elastic and stand in a warm place, 70°F (20°C), for ten days, stirring daily. Strain into fermenting jar and fit air lock. Ferment until the wine clears and fermentation slows. Rack into a clean jar and refit lock. Rack again after three months into clean bottles and cork down.

Rose Hip Syrup

Rose hip syrup provides an easy way of making wine, and a 6 fl oz (170 ml) bottle is sufficient to make 5 quarts (4.5 liters). Common brands in the UK are Delrosa, in 6 fl oz (170 ml) and 12 fl oz (340 ml) sizes, and Optrose, in a 6 fl oz (170 ml) size.

You can also buy black currant and rose hip syrup, and orange and rose hip syrup, which can be used for winemaking in exactly the same way as straight rose hip syrup.

Ingredients

- 6 fl oz, 170 ml (1 small bottle) rose hip syrup
- 2.2 lb (1 kg) sugar
- 112 fl oz (3.5 liters) water
- ¼ oz (10 g) citric acid
- Yeast and nutrient

Method

Merely bring the water to the boil, add the syrup and sugar, and stir well to dissolve. When cool, 70°F (20°C), add the citric acid, yeast, and nutrient and stir again. Pour into fermenting jar and fit airlock, leaving in a warm place to ferment. After a week or so, top up to bottom of neck with cold boiled water and refit lock. Ferment, rack, and bottle in usual way.

ROSEMARY WINE

(Rosmarinus officinalis)

"There's rosemary, that's for remembrance."
Shakespeare

INGREDIENTS

- 1 small packet rosemary herb
- ½ oz (15 g) citric acid (or 3 lemons, no pith, in lieu)
- 3 lb (1.3 kg) sugar
- A pinch of grape tannin
- 5 fl oz (150 ml) grape concentrate
- Yeast nutrient and activated wine yeast
- Water to 5 quarts (4.5 liters)

METHOD

Pour 112 fl oz (3.5 liters) of boiling water over the rosemary herb and infuse as for tea. Strain onto sugar and stir to dissolve. When cool, add the grape tannin, citric acid, and grape concentrate. When cooled again, add the yeast nutrient and activated wine yeast. Fit air lock to fermenting vessel and leave until it clears. Rack and bottle in due course (three-quarters of a month later).

Sauternes

P. Duncan and B. Acton

Ingredients

- 2 lb (1 kg) bananas
- 3 lb (1.3 kg) ripe gooseberries or apricots
  (or tin of apricot pulp)
- 16 fl oz (500 ml) white grape concentrate
- 10 fl oz (280 ml) elderflowers or a packet of dried flowers
- 1 fl oz (30 ml) glycerol (obtained at any chemist as glycerin)
- $\frac{1}{10}$ oz (5 g) tannin
- Sauternes yeast (or wine yeast of choice) and yeast nutrient
- Sugar syrup as required, made by boiling 2 lb (1 kg) sugar with
  16 fl oz (500 ml) water.
- Acid as required to produce acidity of 5.2 parts per thousand sulfur or, if not using
  acid testing kit, between ¼ oz and ¾ oz (10 g and 25 g) acid (equal parts malic acid
  and tartaric acid or a citric/malic/tartaric mixture). Riper fruit will require the
  addition of more acid than less ripe fruit.
- Water to 5 quarts (4.5 liters)

Method

Peel bananas and boil (with skins) in 1 quart (1 liter) of water for half an hour.
Put concentrate, fruit, and flowers in a plastic bucket and strain boiling liquor
from bananas over them. When cool, bring liquid content up to 112 fl oz
(3.5 liters) by adding about 27 fl oz (800 ml) cold water. Add ¼ oz (10 g) citric
acid, tannin, glycerol, and nutrient. Add a vigorously fermenting yeast starter.
After three days, strain off fruit and continue fermentation in a fermenting jar
or other container closed with an air lock. Add 5 fl oz (150 ml) doses of sugar
syrup whenever wine goes dry or gravity drops to below 1010. If fermentation
proceeds longer than eight weeks, make a preliminary racking with plenty of
splashing to aerate the wine and add further nutrients to continue fermentation
to its final point. When fermentation ceases, rack and sulfate to 100 parts per
million with two Campden tablets per 5 quarts (4.5 liters). Mature for at least a
year, preferably in a cask, racking every three months and sulfating each time to
50 parts per million or one Campden tablet.

SHERRY

(Dry Fino type)

P. Duncan and B. Acton

INGREDIENTS

* 1 lb (450 g) bananas
* 20 fl oz (570 ml) white grape concentrate
* ½ oz (15 g) tartaric acid
* 1 oz (30 g) gypsum (calcium sulfate)
* Sugar to be added as below
* 2 lb (1 kg) parsnips, turnips, or carrots
* ½ oz (15 g) cream of tartar
* Good sherry yeast culture and yeast nutrient
* Pectic enzyme
* Water to 5 quarts (4.5 liters)

METHOD

Peel bananas, chop root vegetables, and boil both in 2.5 quarts (2 liters) of water for half an hour. Strain liquor over grape concentrate, tartaric acid, and cream of tartar. Stir until latter dissolves. When cool, add gypsum and yeast nutrient with vigorous stirring. Adjust gravity of must with syrup and water until you have 5 quarts (4.5 liters) at a gravity measuring between 1110 and 1120. (You will need about 3 lb (1.35 kg) sugar and 1.5 quarts (1.5 liters) water to reach this measurement.) Add yeast and pectic enzyme and endeavor to obtain a long cool fermentation lasting up to two months.

Rack carefully into a container large enough to ensure a good air space above the wine and plug container with cotton wool. Keep in a temperature of 55°-65°F (13°-17°C) undisturbed by any movement for at least one year. If a flor forms, tasting must be done by carefully cutting a small hole in the yeast skin.

SHERRY

(Oloroso type)

P. Duncan and B. Acton

INGREDIENTS

- 2 lb (1 kg) bananas
- 3 lb (1.3 kg) peaches
- 1 lb (450 g) chopped raisins
- ½ oz (15 g) tartaric acid
- Sherry wine yeast culture and yeast nutrient
- Sugar syrup to be added as below (syrup made by boiling up 2 lb (1 kg) sugar with 20 fl oz (570 ml) water).

METHOD

Peel bananas and boil in 2.5 quarts (2 liters) of water for half an hour. Strain boiling water over raisins and peaches. Mix in tartaric acid and leave to cool for twelve hours. Add nutrient and a vigorously fermenting yeast starter. Ferment on pulp for three days, then strain off pulp into 5-quart (4.5 liter) jar, pressing fruit lightly. Bring volume up to 136 fl oz (4 liters). Check gravity periodically and add 5 fl oz (150 ml) doses of sugar syrup every time the gravity falls to 1005.

When fermentation is complete, rack very carefully and place in container larger than amount of wine, allowing good air space, and plug with cotton wool plug only. Leave in a warm place (around 75°F, 25°C) for at least three months (or longer if temperature is cooler than this). A flor should not normally develop in this case, but a good sherry flavor will result.

Sweeten to taste when bottling.

Both the sherry recipes are better if the minimum quantity of 15-17.5 quarts (13.5-16 liters) is made.

SLOE WINE

INGREDIENTS

- 3 lb (1.3 kg) sloes
- ½ lb (225 g) raisins
- 3 lb (1.3 kg) sugar
- 112 fl oz (3.5 liters) water
- Yeast and nutrient

METHOD

Mash the sloes well, pour over them the boiling water, and then add the minced raisins and 2 lb (1 kg) of sugar. Stir well and cool to 70°F (20°C). Add yeast, cover with a cloth, and leave to ferment in a warm room for ten days. Strain onto remaining sugar and pour into fermenting jar. Thereafter, continue as in elderberry recipe. If the wine is a little too bitter towards the end of the fermentation, as it may be, a little more sugar can be added (4 oz (100 g) at a time). Usually such additions will be unnecessary. The remarks about color loss and maturing time apply equally to sloe as to elderberry. A blend of two-thirds elderberry, one-third sloe is usually about right if these recipes are used, but each is an excellent wine in its own right.

Table Wine
(Red, dry)

P. Duncan and B. Acton

Ingredients

* 12 lb (5 kg) elderberries or 3½ lb (1.6 kg) dried elderberries
* 6 lb (3 kg) raisins
* 7 lb (3.5 kg) sugar
* Acid (preferably ⅓ malic, ⅓ citric, ⅓ tartaric) mixture 8 level tablespoons
* Yeast and yeast nutrient
* Water to 22.5 quarts (20 liters)

Method

Crush elderberries and chop raisins. Add 15 quarts (13.5 liters) cold water plus three Campden tablets. After twenty-four hours, add yeast nutrient and an actively fermenting yeast starter. Ferment on pulp for a further two days, stirring pulp into the must twice daily. Then strain off the pulp and press lightly. Add all the sugar in the form of syrup. Make up total quantity to 22.5 quarts (20 liters) with water and add acid. Ferment to dryness and rack into a cask. Rack initially four months later and then as required by cask conditions. The wine should remain in cask for fifteen to eighteen months, after which it can be bottled and should remain in bottle for twelve months before consumption. It should by this time have acquired a pleasant character, possibly reminiscent of a burgundy, with an alcohol content of 12.5 percent by volume.

TANGERINE WINE

INGREDIENTS

- 12-15 tangerines
- 2 lb, 11 oz (1.2 kg) sugar
- Yeast and nutrient
- Water to 5 quarts (4.5 liters)

METHOD

Peel the tangerines and crush them by hand. Discard the peel. Pour 112 fl oz
(3.5 liters) of boiling water over the crushed fruit and leave it to soak for twelve
hours. Strain. Warm the juice. Pour over the sugar and stir until all is dissolved.
Cool to 70°F (20°C) and add the yeast (a wine yeast or a level teaspoon of
granulated yeast). Pour into fermentation jar and fit trap. When ferment slows,
top up with cold water. Ferment until finished and the wine is clear. Then rack
into clean bottles.

"Some of these old recipes use large quantities..."

Tansy Wine
(Tanacetum vulgare)

Ingredients

- 1 small packet tansy herb
- 3 lb (1.3 kg) parsnips
- 3 lb (1.3 kg) sugar
- ½ oz (15 g) citric acid (or 3 lemons, no pith, in lieu)
- A pinch of grape tannin
- Sufficient water to produce 5 quarts (4.5 liters) must
- Yeast nutrient and activated wine yeast

Method

Scrub the parsnips, then slice them thinly and boil in 96 fl oz (3 liters) of water until just tender, but not mushy. Strain the liquid onto the sugar and stir until dissolved. Next, pour 20 fl oz (600 ml) of boiling water over the tansy herb and infuse as in making tea. When cool, add the tansy infusion, citric acid, and cold tea to the sweetened parsnip extract. Add the yeast nutrient and activated wine yeast and ferment under an air lock in the normal way. The tansy herb should be used sparingly as it is rather hot, yet at the same time pleasant and aromatic. It is used often in lieu of ginger.

"...but I only drink a gallon of it a day..."

GREEN TOMATO WINE
C. Shave

INGREDIENTS

- 3 lb (1.3 kg) green tomatoes
- 1 quart (1 liter) balm leaves, including stalks
- 1 lb (450 g) raisins, sultanas, or currants
- 1 lb (450 g) corn, barley, or wheat
- 2 lemons or oranges (or ½ oz (15 g) citric acid)
- 3 lb (1.3 kg) sugar
- A pinch of grape tannin
- Activated yeast and nutrient
- Water to 5 quarts (4.5 liters)

METHOD

Soak the grains overnight in a little extra water. Scald the dried fruit and pass the grains, leaves, and stalks together with the tomatoes, dried fruit, and fruit rinds (no white pith) through a mincer. Place the minced ingredients in the fermenting jar and add the sugar. Pour 96 fl oz (3 liters) boiling water over this and stir well to dissolve the sugar. When cool, add the cold tea, fruit juices or citric acid, activated yeast, and nutrient. Ferment for seven days, then strain into a glass jar, topping up to bottom of neck with cold water. Fit air lock, ferment, and rack in the normal way.

Yarrow Wine
(Achillea Millefolium)

Also known as milfoil, yarrow is a weed found in pastures, roadside wastes, and on commons. In winemaking, the flowers and bruised leaves (no stalk) are used. The yarrow flowers from June to the end of the year.

Ingredients

- 5 quarts (4.5 liters) yarrow flowers and bruised leaves
- 1 lb (450 g) chopped raisins
- 2.2 lb (1 kg) sugar
- A pinch of grape tannin
- 2 oranges
- 2 lemons (or ½ oz (15 g) citric acid)
- Activated yeast and nutrient
- Water to 5 quarts (4.5 liters)

Method

Remove the blooms and put them into a bowl with the chopped raisins. Pour 112 fl oz (3.5 liters) of boiling water over them and leave to soak for four or five days. Strain into a pan and add the thinly peeled skins of the oranges (no white pith) and the sugar. Simmer for twenty minutes. Add the juice of the oranges and lemons (or citric acid) and the tea. Stir, then strain immediately into a bowl or polythene bucket. Allow to cool to 70°F (20°C). Add yeast and nutrient. Keep well covered in a warm place for seven days until the first vigorous ferment has died down, then transfer to a fermenting jar and fit a fermentation lock. Top up to bottom of neck with cold water if necessary. Wait until all fermentation has ceased (usually about two months), then rack for the first time. A second racking two or three months later will be beneficial if a second yeast deposit forms. This time your yarrow wine can be bottled. Keep it at least six months before you drink it.

Elderberry and Bilberry Wines

Elderberries are excellent for making the Englishman's port, as the wine from them is sometimes called. Indeed, at one time, until the practice was made illegal in the UK, elderberries were used to improve true port. Some winemakers are occasionally disappointed in their elderberry wine because it seems unduly harsh and dry, so much so as to be almost undrinkable young, but if the wine is matured sufficiently (sometimes it needs two years) this harshness, caused by the excess tannin in this fruit, disappears. If you cannot resist drinking your elderberry wine young, the addition of a little sugar just before use effects a near-miraculous improvement.

In all the following recipes, whether for fresh or dried fruit, bilberries can be substituted for elderberries. They too make a glorious wine, the flavor of which many prefer to that of the elderberry.

Ecstatic Elderberry (Basic Recipe)

Ingredients

- 4 lb (2 kg) elderberries
- 2 lb, 11 oz (1.2 kg) sugar
- Burgundy yeast (or wine yeast of choice) and nutrient
- ½ oz (15 g) citric acid
- Water to 5 quarts (4.5 liters)

Method

To strip the berries from the stalks, wear rubber gloves or use the prongs of a fork or steel comb. Otherwise, it is a messy and tedious business. Be careful that drops of the juice do not stain your clothes, because the mark seems to resist all subsequent attempts to remove it. Weigh the berries (together with any other fruit recommended in the variation recipes) and crush them in a bowl or bucket. If grape concentrate is being used, add it at this stage. Pour on 112 fl oz (3.5 liters) of boiling water, stir well, and allow to cool to 70°F (20°C) before adding the yeast, acid, and nutrient. Cover closely and leave for three days in a warm place, stirring daily, then strain through a nylon sieve onto the sugar. Pour the liquor into a stone jar or dark glass jar (in clear bottles the wine will lose its glorious ruby color), but do not fill completely until the first vigorous ferment has subsided. When it has, top up with cold boiled water and fit fermentation lock. Leave till fermentation is complete, then siphon off into clean dark bottles (if you have no dark bottles, cover your white ones with a sugar bag or brown paper, or keep them in a dark cupboard) and keep for a further six months at least.

ELDERBERRY ENCHANT

INGREDIENTS

- 4 lb (2 kg) elderberries
- 2¾ lb (1.2 kg) white sugar
- 5 fl oz (150 ml) grape concentrate
- ½ oz (15 g) citric acid
- Wine yeast culture and nutrient
- Water to 5 quarts (4.5 liters)

METHOD

As for Ecstatic Elderberry on page 116, except that grape concentrate is added to the must. This gives a slightly stronger wine with a more vinous nose.

NON PAREIL
(from a French recipe)

INGREDIENTS

- 3 lb (1.3 kg) elderberries
- 1 lb (450 g) damsons
- 2¾ lb (1.2 kg) sugar
- ½ oz (15 g) citric acid
- Wine yeast culture and nutrient
- Water to 5 quarts (4.5 liters)

METHOD

Use the same basic method as Ecstatic Elderberry on page 116.

Ambrosia
(an eighteenth-century recipe)

Ingredients

- 3 lb (1.3 kg) elderberries
- 1 lb (450 g) raisins
- Root ginger and cloves
- 2¾ lb (1.2 kg) sugar
- ½ oz (15 g) citric acid
- Wine yeast culture and nutrient

Method

Boil the root ginger and cloves in the water while bringing it to the boil. Simmer for fifteen minutes. Add the stoned raisins, then continue as indicated in Ecstatic Elderberry on page 116. The inclusion of the root ginger and cloves is optional and may be omitted if desired, but was greatly liked in olden days, when spicy flavors were popular.

Crème De Raisin

Ingredients

- 3 lb (1.3 kg) elderberries
- 4 lb (2 kg) grapes (or 16 fl oz (500 ml) grape concentrate)
- 2¼ lb (about 1 kg) sugar
- ½ oz (15 g) citric acid
- Wine yeast culture and nutrient

Method

Use the same basic method as Ecstatic Elderberry on page 116.

VINO MAGNIFICO

INGREDIENTS

- 3 lb (1.3 kg) elderberries
- 1 lb (450 g) sloes
- 5 fl oz (150 ml) grape concentrate
- 2¼ lb (about 1 kg) sugar
- ½ oz (15 g) citric acid
- Wine yeast culture and nutrient

METHOD

Use the same basic method as Ecstatic Elderberry on page 116.

ELDERBERRY AND APPLE

INGREDIENTS

- 3 lb (1.3 kg) elderberries
- 4 lb (2 kg) apples
- 2¼ lb (about 1 kg) sugar
- ½ oz (15 g) citric acid
- Yeast culture and nutrient

METHOD

Wash and cut up the apples and boil ten to fifteen minutes in 136 fl oz (4 liters) of water; then strain onto elderberries and proceed as for Ecstatic Elderberry on page 116.

As You Like It

Ingredients

- 2 lb (1 kg) elderberries
- 2 lb (1 kg) blackberries
- 2½ lb (1.2 kg) sugar
- 1 oz (30 g) citric acid
- Wine yeast culture and nutrient

Method

Use the same basic method as Ecstatic Elderberry on page 116.

Aromatic Splendor

Ingredients

- 4 lb (2 kg) elderberries
- About 1 quart (1 liter) commercial cider (or more)
- ½ oz (15 g) citric acid
- Yeast culture and nutrient
- 2 lb (1 kg) sugar

Method

Reduce the amount of water being used by the amount of cider added and proceed as for Ecstatic Elderberry on page 116.

HERBAL NECTAR

INGREDIENTS

- 1 oz (30 g) mixed herbs
- 4 lb (2 kg) elderberries
- ½ oz (15 g) citric acid
- Yeast culture and nutrient

METHOD

Use the same basic method as Ecstatic Elderberry on page 116.

ELDERBERRY WINE
(from dried elderberries or bilberries)

INGREDIENTS

- 1 lb (450 g) dried elderberries (equal to 4 1b, (2 kg) fresh fruit)
- 2¼ lb (about 1 kg) sugar
- 6.75 fl oz (200 ml) grape concentrate
- 1 lemon
- Yeast and yeast nutrient
- Water to 5 quarts (4.5 liters)

METHOD

Bring 136 fl oz (4 liters) of water to the boil and pour over the dried elderberries. Put this, 1 lb (450 g) sugar, concentrate, and lemon juice in polythene bucket. Stir well and cover. Allow to cool to 70°F (20°C), then add the yeast and yeast nutrient. A bordeaux, port, or burgundy yeast is excellent. Ferment on the pulp for a week before straining through a nylon sieve or muslin into the fermenting jar, add remaining sugar, and make up to 5 quarts (4.5 liters). Stir well to dissolve. Fit an air lock and ferment in the usual way. Rack for the first time when the wine clears and again three months later.

The same recipe can be used for bilberries.

Concentrated Fruit Juices

Several readers have asked for recipes for using some of the fruit juice concentrates now available, so here are some they may care to try:

Cider or Perry

Gravity 1060, 25 quarts (22.5 liters): Use 5 quarts (4.5 liters) concentrated apple or pear juice. Use a reliable yeast nutrient and wine yeast.

Light Apple or Pear Wine

Gravity 1100, 25 quarts (22.5 liters): Use 5 quarts (4.5 liters) concentrated apple or pear juice, 15 quarts (13.5 liters) water, and 5 lb, 6 oz (2.4 kg) sugar dissolved initially in 112 fl oz (2.8 liters) water. Use a good yeast nutrient and wine yeast.

HEAVY SWEET APPLE OR PEAR WINE

Gravity 1150: Use 5 quarts (4.5 liters) of concentrated apple or pear juice plus 12.5 quarts (11 liters) of water. First make a syrup by dissolving 12 lb (5.5 kg) of sugar in 112 fl oz (3.5 liters) of the water. Add one-third of this syrup to the must and ferment with wine yeast and a good nutrient. Add the remainder of the syrup in two doses at suitable intervals, when the fermentation slows. To make 5 quarts (4.5 liters), adjust ingredients accordingly.

CYSER (MELOMEL)

Substitute 20 fl oz (570 ml) apple juice concentrate for 1 lb (450 g) honey per 5 quarts (4.5 liters) in any mead recipe and reduce any added acid recommended by at least ¼ oz (10 g) per 5 quarts (4.5 liters).

RHUBARB AND APPLE

Substitute 20 fl oz (570 ml) concentrate for 1 lb (450 g) of sugar per 5 quarts (4.5 liters) in any rhubarb recipe and reduce any added acid recommended by at least ¼ oz (10 g) per 5 quarts (4.5 liters).

Christmas Drinks

Old-Time Punch
Makes ten wine glasses.

INGREDIENTS
- 1 bottle of any red wine
- 1 cup granulated sugar
- 2 level tablespoons honey
- 1 lemon
- Little grated nutmeg
- 16 fl oz (500 ml) hot water
- 2 sliced oranges
- 1 carefully peeled red apple

METHOD
Heat wine with sugar, honey, sliced lemon rounds, and grated nutmeg in pan to near boiling point. Add the hot water. Pour over sliced orange and apple rounds in large bowl. Decorate with whole length of apple peel.

Spiced Cider Comforter
Makes eight wine glasses.

INGREDIENTS
- 6 level tablespoons honey
- 1 bottle vintage cider
- Small stick cinnamon
- 1 lemon

METHOD
Dissolve honey gently in cider over low heat, add cinnamon, lemon peel, and juice. Serve hot.

Wine Cup

Ingredients

- 1 bottle red country wine
- 1 lemon (juice only)
- 4 fl oz (150 ml) gin
- 8 oz (250 ml) sherry
- 1 siphon soda water

Method

Mix all the ingredients together. Garnish with slices of cucumber, a sprig of mint, and enrich with maraschino cherries and a little maraschino liqueur if desired. The cup should be served roughly at room temperature and should not be allowed to stand longer than necessary.

Che-Na-Grum

In Cornwall, England, a favorite Christmas drink is Che-na-grum, or She-nac-rum, which is hot sweetened beer flavored with rum, grated nutmeg, and sometimes ginger, and garnished with slices of lemon.

Method

Place two lumps of sugar in a tumbler. Add a wineglass of rum. Fill up the glass with hot boiled beer and float two slices of lemon on top. (Enough for one person.)

WASSAIL BOWL

INGREDIENTS

- 60 fl oz (1.75 liters) ale
- ½ lb (225 g) brown sugar
- ½ bottle sherry
- 6 roasted apples
- ½ oz (60 g) ground ginger
- ½ grated nutmeg
- Pinch of ground cinnamon
- 2 lumps of sugar
- 1 washed lemon
- ½ lemon

METHOD

Prepare the apples first. Core them, stuff with brown sugar, and roast in a covered dish for twenty minutes, then uncover, baste, and finish cooking. Mix the spices with the sugar. Place in an enamel saucepan. Add 16 fl oz (500 ml) ale. Stir over low heat till dissolved, then bring to boil. Draw pan to side of stove. Stir in remainder of ale, the sherry, and the sugar, rubbed onto the lemon until all the oil is extracted. Heat till piping hot, but do not allow to boil. Pour into a hot ornamental bowl. Add the hot roasted stuffed apples, then the half lemon, peeled so that all the white pith has been removed, and cut in slices. Place the bowl on a cake board or salver and ornament round the base with holly or mistletoe. Serve at once with a ladle.

ALE PUNCH

INGREDIENTS

- 2 oz (55 g) castor sugar
- 1 lemon
- 2 quarts (2 liters) light ale
- 8 fl oz (250 ml) sherry
- 6 trays of ice

METHOD

Place the sugar in a punch bowl. Wash the lemon. Remove rind as thinly as possible and add to sugar. Extract lemon juice and strain over the sugar. Stand for thirty minutes, then remove lemon rind. Add ale, sherry, and ice. Garnish with one or two slices of lemon. (Enough for six or seven people.)

"...and now a few words about mead..."

BEERS AND STOUTS

MORGAN'S ALE

INGREDIENTS

- 1 lb (450 g) malt extract
- ½ lb (225 g) sugar
- 1 oz (30 g) hops (or to taste)
- Yeast
- Water to 5 quarts (4.5 liters)

METHOD

Boil up the ingredients in 2.5 quarts (2 liters) of water in pressure cooker for thirty minutes. Strain, add 2.5 quarts (2 liters) of cold water and yeast. Set aside to ferment, closely covered, and skim off the cap every twenty-four hours. When fermentation has apparently ceased (usually about a week), bottle in 1-quart (1 liter) beer bottles, adding a level teaspoon of sugar to each bottle. Cork tightly and seal with crown caps or screw stoppers, Stand in a cool place to clear. The beer is usually ready to drink after another two weeks.

"If my wife knew I had as much as this, she'd have half the village down here, sampling…"

Berrybrew: a strong bitter

Ingredients

- 4 lb (2 kg) malt extract
- 4 lb (2 kg) sugar
- 3 oz (100 g) hops
- 2 tablespoons gravy browning
- 1 level teaspoon citric acid
- 2 teaspoons salt
- 22.5 quarts (20 liters) water
- Yeast

Method

Put hops, salt, and gravy browning (which is only caramel coloring) into some or all of the water (I use 12.5 quarts, 11 liters), making sure you have a few extra hops to add later. If preferred, you can add the ingredients to a muslin bag and place the bag in the water. Bring to the boil. Simmer for forty minutes. Add a few loose hops and simmer for a further five minutes.

Meanwhile, stand the jars of malt extract in hot water for ten minutes to facilitate pouring, then put the malt extract and sugar into a polythene bin and strain the hopped wort onto them. Stir well to dissolve and add the acid. Make up to the desired quantity with the remainder of the water (10-15 quarts, 9-13.5 liters) cold. (If using a carboy for fermentation, the whole of the wort thus prepared can be poured into carboy when cool.)

Allow to cool to 70°F (20°C) and then add a good brewer's yeast and nutrient. Use proprietary yeasts in quantities recommended. With granulated yeast, use 3 level teaspoons. Close the bin with a polythene sheet secured with elastic (or, if carboy, with air lock). Fermentation should be vigorous in thirty-six hours and complete in ten days.

When the surface of the beer has cleared and only tiny bubbles are visible in a ring in the center (the gravity must be 1010 or below, and preferably down to 1000-1002), bottle in strong 1-quart (1 liter) beer or cider bottles. Fill to within ½ in (1 cm) of bottom of stopper, add 1 level teaspoon of white sugar to each bottle (not more), and screw down hard. Put the beer in a cool (not cold) place, and it will be clear and ready for drinking after two weeks or so.

Boys' Bitter

Ingredients

- 1 lb (450 g) malt extract
- 1 oz (30 g) hops
- 5 quarts (4.5 liters) water
- Yeast

Method

This is an excellent basic beer, and its bitterness can be adjusted by increasing or decreasing the amount of hops proportionately. Since it is ready to drink after just over a week, you can experiment with two or three consecutive gallons and get the flavor to your personal taste before multiplying the quantities to make the beer in bulk. While experimenting, pay regard principally to flavor rather than to clarity. To obtain complete clarity, it is necessary to store the beer in a cool place for a month.

Bring the water to the boil, add the malt extract and hops, and simmer for an hour and a half. Top up to the original volume with more water, then strain through muslin or close-mesh flour sieve into a large fermenting bin or vessel. (If you use normal 5-quart (4.5 liter) fermentation jars, they must not be filled beyond the shoulder because of the froth, so use several.)

Add your yeast and keep in a warm place, 70°F (20°C), for four days. Siphon the beer off the yeast deposit into strong bottles. Add a cube of sugar to each bottle and tie down the cork. (It is best not to use screw stoppers until you have really mastered the art of brewing. A tied-down cork will always give warning of impending disaster, a screw-stopper will not.) Move the beer into a cool place. It will be drinkable in another week.

OATMEAL STOUT

INGREDIENTS

* ¾ lb (350 g) rye
* ½ lb (225 g) black malt
* ½ lb (225 g) pale malt
* 5 oz (150 g) oatmeal
* 2 oz (55 g) hops
* 4 lb (2 kg) sugar
* 20 quarts (18 liters) water

METHOD

Crack the pale malt (but not the black) with a rolling pin and put all the malt into about 10 quarts (9 liters) of water at 150°F (60°C) in a 10-quart (9 liter) bucket. Then insert a 50-watt glass immersion heater (such as is used in tropical fish tanks), wrap the bucket in a blanket or thick cloth, and leave the heater switched on for a period of eight hours; this can conveniently be done overnight. This will maintain the brew at the ideal temperature for mashing (150°F or 65°C) and extraction will be first-rate. Pour into a boiler and add the hops, rye, and oatmeal, and boil for an hour, adding a few extra hops in the last five minutes. Strain into the fermenting vessel onto the sugar and make up to just over 20 quarts (18 liters) with cold water. Cool to 75°F (25°C) before adding the yeast and fermenting in the usual way. When the surface of the wort begins to clear and bubbles are collecting centrally (or when the gravity is nearing 1001) bottle, adding 1 level teaspoon of sugar to each quart (1 liter) beer bottle. Store in a cool dark place until the homebrew clears, and pour out carefully and steadily to avoid disturbing sediment.

If you cannot obtain an immersion heater to do the extraction properly, all the ingredients (except, of course, the yeast) can be simmered in all, or some, of the water, the sugar added, and the wort then fermented, but the resultant stout will not be of quite such high quality,

Seward Ale: 25-quart (22.5 liter) recipe

Ingredients

- 25 quarts (22.5 liters) water
- 1½ lb (675 g) brown sugar
- 1½ oz (45 g) crushed barley
- 1 lb (1 kg) brown malt extract
- 3 oz (90 g) hops
- Yeast

Method

Soak the barley in a little water overnight and run it through a mincer. Boil the hops (the packaged variety will do), malt (obtainable from homebrew stores or online), and barley for thirty minutes in 10 quarts (9 liters) of the water. Strain onto the sugar and stir to dissolve it, then add the remaining water (cold). Allow to cool to about 70°F (20°C), then add yeast (a good beer yeast or a level teaspoon of granulated yeast). Cover closely and allow to ferment in a warm place for forty-eight hours, skimming frequently. By then the gravity should have dropped to about 1010. Bottle without disturbing the sediment by using a siphon tube. Keep the beer another five or six days in a cool place, after which it can be drunk, but it will be vastly improved for being left another three weeks. If a darker beer is required (this one is light in color) add up to ½ oz (15 g) licorice to the 25 quarts (22.5 liters).

INDEX

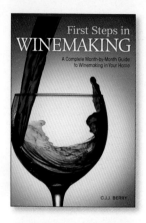
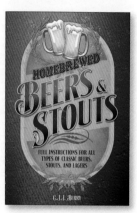
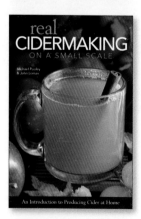